THE DOUGLAS YEARS

THE DOUGLAS YEARS

DEDICATED TO THE
PEOPLE OF VERMONT

James H. Douglas
Governor of Vermont
2003 – 2011

2011

Printed in the United States of America.
Not printed at government expense.

Cover design by Scott C. Hampton

– First Edition –
ISBN: 978-0-615-47992-7
Library of Congress Control Number: 2011927898

The Fourteenth Star Press
South Burlington, Vermont

73 TH SY NL DC JG TP DC II

To the people of Vermont, thank you for the unparalleled opportunity to serve as your governor. Public service is a privilege and the faith you have placed in me is humbling.

To the members of my cabinet and staff, thank you for answering my call to service and fulfilling your obligations with the highest degree of professionalism and dedication. Your hard work, ideas and counsel have been indispensable.

And to Dorothy, simply put, this journey would not have been possible without your love and support. Thank you, my dear.

THE DOUGLAS YEARS

APPENDIX

Selected Photographs
91

Selected Major Speeches

First Inaugural Address
106

2004 State of the State
114

Second Inaugural Address
127

2006 State of the State
136

Third Inaugural Address
152

2008 State of the State
164

Fourth Inaugural Address
177

2010 State of the State
194

Not Seeking a Fifth Term
210

That all power being originally inherent in and consequently derived from the people, therefore, all officers of government, whether legislative or executive, are their trustees and servants; and at all times, in a legal way, accountable to them.

Article 6
Vermont Constitution

THE DOUGLAS YEARS

Vision

"I love Vermont...I want every Vermonter to reach his or her highest potential. I want every child to begin life in good health, with a loving family, and eager to learn. I want every young Vermonter to be able to access a higher education and to secure meaningful and rewarding work. I want families to be able to afford a home and ultimately to enjoy retirement in comfort and dignity..."
— Why I Want to Run for Governor, 2001 —

WHEN I DECIDED to pursue the governor's office in the spring of 2001, I sat down and put my reasons for doing so in writing. I carried that piece of paper with me every day as a reminder of what this job means, not to me personally, but to the people I have been so privileged to serve. After nearly 30 years as a legislator, secretary of state and state treasurer, I was confident in my ability to chart a course for our state that adhered to the goals and aspirations of Vermonters.

I knew I could not do it alone – no one could. A governor sets ambitious objectives, recruits the best and the brightest and leads Vermonters in a dialogue through which they develop ownership in the state's policies and goals. I believe that I lived up to that standard and I am thankful to all who helped along the way. The job of governor is more than running the machinery of state government and setting policy. A governor sets an example and leads. Through every debate – no matter how contentious– I sought to uphold the Vermont tradition of dignified civil discourse. I worked to bring people together around shared goals and, when differences could not be bridged, never faulted others for sincerely held convictions. In a time of searing political rhetoric, the way we conduct our public business here in Vermont is something of which we should rightly be proud.

After eight years as governor, countless miles traveled across our state and thousands and thousands of conversations with Vermonters from all walks of life, I am proud of the difference we made. Vermont is the healthiest state and the greenest state. After the nation's deepest recession in generations, we have among the lowest unemployment rates, the highest bond ratings and the least stressed economies of any state in America. Our communities are safer from drugs and violent criminals. Our infrastructure is better maintained and funded. We achieved groundbreaking reforms in health care, making us a leader among states. We protected our natural gifts – our waterways, our air, our forests and our wildlife. We allowed for greater certainty within our permitting system. We brought state government into the 21st century and supported our next generation in their pursuit of higher education and quality jobs.

But success is not rankings alone. Indeed, the initiatives we started and advanced will evolve and change. New technologies and new ideas will allow for new opportunities. Unforeseen challenges will emerge. But what endures – the legacy that is left – is found in the lives and stories of the people of this great state.

It is found in the story of a mother who, because of our *Choices for Care* program, could now care for her daughter at home, when she would have otherwise been forced into a nursing home by a debilitating medical condition.

It is found in the story of a high school graduate who was able to pay for college with the help of a *Next Generation Scholarship* and can now pursue his aspirations.

It is found in the story of a woman who could go back to work and again enjoy life after getting control of her chronic illness with help from her community health team as a result of our *Blueprint for Health*.

It is found in the story of a small business owner whose dream of growing his company was aided by the *Vermont Employment Growth Incentive*, allowing him to create new jobs for fellow Vermonters.

It is found in the story of a local organization bringing farmers, sportsmen and other residents together to tackle the difficult problem of phosphorous in our waterways.

It is found in the story that fortunately does not have to be told because a young Vermonter made the right choice when confronted with drugs.

And it is on full display when we welcome home the brave men and women of our National Guard after they have given a year of their lives and precious time away from their families in service to our state and nation.

It has been an honor and a privilege to be there with Vermonters in their times of triumph and in times of adversity – working side-by-side to help build an even better tomorrow. It is in these extraordinary stories of Vermonters that I have been inspired to work as hard as I can every day.

A More Prosperous People

"Although this current volatility is caused by national ailments far removed from the Green Mountains, we are not immune to its effects. But because of smart choices we made over the last five years, Vermont is better positioned than most states to weather this storm and break through stronger still."
— Seventh Budget Message, 2009 —

VERMONT IS NOT an island. The eight years I served as governor were volatile times economically for the national and world economies. More importantly, it was a challenging time for Vermonters working hard to make a living for themselves and their families. It was a period that saw two recessions – including the deepest downturn since the Depression – as well as significant advances in technology that led to new opportunities and demands.

Vermont weathered these economic upheavals better than most. Unemployment, while high as a result of the Great Recession, is among the lowest in the nation. And, according to one analysis, by the end of 2010, we were among the least economically stressed states in America.

Early Downturn, Quick Recovery

The recession of the early 2000's officially lasted from March 2000 to October 2001. However, Vermonters saw rising unemployment and job insecurity well after the economists determined that the national economy turned the corner. Unemployment peaked at 4.5 percent and stayed there for the first eight months of my term in office in 2003.

I hosted Regional Jobs Summits in every corner of the state during my transition and my early weeks in office to solicit ideas to fight back against the flagging economy. Those discussions with Vermonters informed the largest jobs package in state history to that time. The $105 million initiative included enhancements to the state's tax credit programs, recapitalization of the Vermont Economic Development Authority so it could provide low-interest capital to Vermont businesses and increased investments in workforce training. Our earlier efforts did not stop with those initiatives.

Between 2003 and 2004, we established a sales tax holiday for computers and increased the minimum wage; encouraged seed capital and angel investments with new incentives and funding; and the top corporate tax rate was reduced by 14 percent – from 9.75 percent to 8.5 percent – moving Vermont from fifth highest in the nation to 16th and making Vermont businesses more competitive.

Our aggressive response helped Vermont recover from the recession faster than the rest of the nation. By November 2004, the state unemployment rate dropped to 3.1 percent, making it the lowest in the nation and 3,400 more Vermonters were back to work.

Smart Incentives for Growing Companies

During that time we also rethought some of our job creation programs. As a small state, Vermont struggles to compete with larger states in offering significant financial incentives to businesses looking to locate or expand here. But that does not mean we should not try to compete, or that we are unable to compete.

The Vermont Economic Progress Council (VEPC) – an independent board that considers applications for various economic incentive programs – is an important tool to create jobs in Vermont. But prior to 2004, the tax credit programs VEPC managed were overly complicated. The very complexity of these programs made them vulnerable to criticism and more difficult to effectively deploy.

My administration crafted a new approach and submitted those ideas to the Legislature in 2004. This dramatic simplification of VEPC's tax credit programs was based on one key performance indicator: job creation. We collapsed all the tax credits into a single, refundable credit a business could claim annually based on meeting job creation targets.

The reforms, enacted in 2006, created the *Vermont Employment Growth Incentive* program (VEGI). Since its creation, 33 companies have qualified and received VEGI credits. Of those, nearly two-thirds are small businesses with fewer than 20 employees. The program also has helped some of Vermont's large employers that drive the economy in regions of our state. By 2010, the program has contributed to the creation of 6,700 direct and indirect jobs in Vermont, adding $20 million in new payroll.

In 2008, I asked the Legislature to enhance the VEGI program by including a new "Green" VEGI incentive. Green VEGI puts an emphasis on environmentally-friendly businesses – building on the Vermont brand of environmental stewardship. To date, VEGI has proved to be one of the most successful job creation tools we have.

More Certainty for Job Creators

Commonsense permit reform was a key part of my economic development strategy. Too often Vermonters become stuck in an uncertain web as they look to expand their enterprise and create jobs. In business, time has value and a clear "yes" or "no" is preferable to "maybe." The goal of permit reform was to provide that greater certainty to employers looking to locate or expand in our state, without compromising our strong environmental standards. A more certain permitting regime would allow for smarter development, greater adherence to the rules and less time and money spent on costly appeals.

I presented my reform ideas in my first Inaugural Address and reiterated my call for legislative action as I travelled the state speaking to Vermonters about the need for removing this key barrier to job creation. After 15 months of work I signed H. 175 into law on May 13, 2004. The reforms updated and modernized the land use permitting system by streamlining the appeals process, while preserving the strict environmental standards we expect. The legislation consolidated the Environmental Board, Water Resources Board, Waste Facility Panel, and the Solid Waste and Air Quality Variance Board into an expanded Environmental Court. The Natural Resources Board was created to handle rulemaking and administrative oversight of the Act 250 District Commissions.

Ultimately, the reforms brought greater clarity on the question of who could be an interested party in a permit proceeding. We eliminated the 11th hour appeal by ensuring that parties must engage in the early stages of the permit process and must have a direct interest. We allowed for appeals to the Supreme Court for aggrieved persons under Act 250. We also made local permitting more timely and efficient by consolidating and updating outdated statutes to improve predictability, reflect current practices and enhance coordination between state and local review processes.

The 2004 reforms were a positive step forward for job creation. But more is still to be done to ensure greater certainty for those who are looking to create jobs. As I have said on many occasions, protecting the environment and growing the economy are not mutually exclusive. Our tough environmental standards are an asset, not a liability. What does impede the achievement of both a healthier environment and vibrant business climate is bureaucratic red tape. Rethinking the state permitting processes, like all processes of state government, is an ongoing endeavor.

Lowering Costs for Employers

Permit reform was, by no means, the only reform needed to make Vermont more jobs-friendly and more competitive. By 2004, Vermont employers had experienced five consecutive years of workers' compensation premium hikes – the latest being nearly 10 percent in 2003. I convened the Governor's Workers' Compensation Advisory Council in 2003 to explore ways in which we could get a handle on these soaring costs.

My administration and the Legislature moved forward in 2004 to enact comprehensive changes to our workers' compensation system. The legislation I signed on May 27, 2004 included many of the reforms supported by the Workers' Compensation Advisory Council, including increased penalties for fraud, a simplified and refined compensation system, mandatory case management for injured workers and other changes to protect the integrity of our workers' compensation system.

In addition to statutory changes, we prioritized workplace wellness and safety. Improving workplace safety is the most effective way to bring down workers' compensation costs. In addition to statutory changes, we enhanced our focus on workplace wellness and safety through the creation and continued support of the Department of Labor's *Workplace Safety Program*. In addition, Project WorkSAFE has been helping employers minimize injuries on the job – allowing for a more efficient workforce and lower workers' compensation costs. We have also promoted worksite wellness and led the way within state government.

Our efforts led to tangible results. In the voluntary market, where more than 90 percent of employers get their coverage, the growth in average cost began to decline from the double-digit increases in 2004. By 2007, average premiums actually began declining, dropping as much as 13 percent in 2009 – the largest decline in more than a decade. For those in the assigned risk market, the market for the most injury-prone industries, rates also improved, dropping every year since 2006. Perhaps more significantly, the number of employers in the assigned risk market declined, signaling a healthy and competitive workers' compensation market.

Of particular note, dairy farms and ski areas – two important and iconic Vermont industries that have historically suffered high workers' compensation costs – have seen premiums drop, at times significantly, in recent years. Although Vermont can continue to improve workers' compensation costs, we are competitive in our region and headed in the right direction nationally.

Our Working Landscape

Agriculture and our forest products economy remain central to our way of life in Vermont. I know that well. For me, agriculture is a family endeavor. My wife, Dorothy, was raised on a farm in Middlebury, where I worked for a time as a young man. That experience gave me a great appreciation for the invigorating lifestyle and hard work.

Dairy alone contributes $2 billion a year to our economy. Yet, it is a rapidly changing industry. The challenges facing farmers are serious. Increased energy and commodity costs combined with declining prices have made it increasingly difficult for many to survive. Dairy farmers, in particular, have been on a rollercoaster as they watched milk prices fall to their lowest levels in a generation – well below the cost of production.

But along with those challenges are new opportunities. Energy development, value-added products, agri-tourism, and a renewed focus on local foods and products hold potential for the industry in the coming years. We sought to cultivate these opportunities, while addressing some of the immediate challenges and encouraging federal reforms necessary to return certainty to this important industry – particularly the dairy sector.

One of the first steps was to provide farmers a bit of relief from the onerous burden of the property tax. Removing buildings on land enrolled in the Current Use program from the property tax was a commonsense change to help those who make a living keeping our working landscape working.

Elevating the Commissioner of Agriculture to Secretary of Agriculture, a cabinet-level position and creating a new Agency of Agriculture, Food and Markets was a foundational step in recognizing the evolving needs of this important sector of our economy.

A strong and growing partnership between agriculture and tourism is one exciting area of progress. Agri-tourism is a growing industry and one that holds great promise. The Department of Tourism and Marketing and Agency of Agriculture have teamed up for numerous initiatives to support agricultural producers, including the successful *Apples to iPods* promotion and events around the Lake Champlain Quadricentennial celebration, where producers and dignitaries from Quebec and Vermont met to exchange ideas and resources.

From artisan cheese producers to our nascent wine industry, we are looking to new opportunities at home and abroad to support our agriculture entrepreneurs. In 2009, I made an official visit to France to learn about and explore the concept of "terroir" – taste of place. We partnered with our friends from Quebec to leverage our brand and exchange ideas on how to promote our Vermont goods and products. My administration also undertook a new effort to revitalize and strengthen the Vermont Seal of Quality in 2010, because we understood the importance of brand integrity. Taking lessons we learned from France and Quebec, the Agency is partnering with industry groups, like dairy and maple producers, to develop strong standards to protect the Vermont brand.

At home, we are encouraging local food production and consumption. Vermont's Farm to School Program has leveraged significant federal resources to link local food producers with schools to provide healthy, local nutrition to young Vermonters. The *Vermont Innovative Kitchens* grants provide support to food producers and entrepreneurs looking to access the infrastructure necessary to make their ventures succeed. I signed legislation to update prohibition-era laws, reflecting the needs of our growing craft brewery and winery industries. And, by 2009, the Mobile Poultry Unit was up and running as the only state inspected mobile processing unit in the country – helping farmers to expand their flocks and reach new markets.

I often bragged to those outside our state that Vermont has the highest number of methane digesters of any state per capita. Electricity from methane digesters is providing a new source of income for farmers, while harnessing a different kind of natural resource for clean energy. In 2006, we became one of the first states to join the *25x'25* initiative, which is an effort to produce 25 percent of the energy consumed in the United States from renewable sources from our forests and farms by the year 2025. And we provided grants through Renewable Energy for Agriculture Program (REAP) to advance renewable technologies on our farms.

Spending time with Vermonters at our county fairs is among the very best parts of summer and fall. The fairs offer every generation an opportunity to learn about and take part in the traditions of our state. I proudly supported the state's fairgrounds and fair organizations, as well as our participation at the Eastern States Exposition in West Springfield, Massachusetts. Our commitment to the Vermont building at that Exposition resulted in increased attendance, vendor participation and revenue – spreading the word about the quality of Vermont products outside our borders.

There are few things we take more seriously in Vermont than the purity of our maple syrup and the strength of our maple industry. As the largest producer of maple syrup in the country, Vermont produced roughly 900 thousand gallons in 2009 and 2010, increasing production by nearly two-fold from 2003. In fact, in 2010, Vermont produced 46 percent of all the maple syrup in America. The demand for quality Vermont maple products, along with the strength of the Vermont brand, will continue to fuel higher demand. To help ensure this iconic Vermont industry can continue to grow, my administration partnered with maple producers to allow for licensing a limited number of sites in state forests and parks to sugarmakers, who abide by state land management policies while operating the sugarbushes.

Although we made significant strides in our agricultural development efforts, national and international forces continue to challenge our working landscape. In 2003, as dairy farmers struggled with low milk prices, I unveiled an emergency financial assistance package designed to provide immediate cash flow relief to Vermont farmers by restructuring existing debt and by making available low-interest loans for spring planting and operating needs. A major component of the package was a *Farm Operating Loan Program* to give farmers direct loans through the Vermont Agricultural Credit Corporation by making available $20 million for loans to help farmers get their crops in the ground.

In 2006, as dairy farmers again confronted low milk prices, high energy costs and bad weather, legislative leaders and I announced a $9 million relief package. In addition to the direct aid for farmers, the package included support for a "Buy Local" campaign, transition funds for organic milk production, and an investment in a farm viability program to help farmers strengthen their business plans and promote profitability.

Another agriculture emergency package was necessary in 2007 as poor weather conditions continued to affect the industry. Legislation was adopted to assist Vermont dairy farmers prevent further loss to the industry. We provided an interim dairy assistance plan where dairy producers received a single payment made by the end of March based on January and February milk production. In the midst of the Great Recession, I announced another program to provide lower-rate operating loans for farmers through the Vermont Economic Development Authority.

Through the Agency of Agriculture we pursued innovative strategies to protect the dairy industry. We teamed up with the University of Vermont and other partners to create the Farms First program, which provides counseling for many concerns like legal and financial assistance, mediation, wellness, eldercare and childcare, disability and disease management, retirement planning, education, and management consultation to help farmers weather uncertain times. The Agency also launched the *Keep Local Farms Program*, which is partnering with institutions and grocery chains throughout New England to highlight the importance of knowing where milk is produced.

Ultimately, the challenge that dairy farmers face in Vermont can only be addressed on a sustainable basis by the federal government. The complicated milk pricing system must be revamped in order to allow Vermonters to compete on a predictable and fair basis with producers across the country.

Welcoming Visitors

Vermont is a state for all seasons. Our working landscapes, mountains, lakes and streams continue to make the Green Mountain State a desired destination for many. From our ski areas to our vibrant downtowns, our state has much to offer.

In fact, in 2007, the World Travel & Tourism Council chose Vermont's downtowns, and the Vermont Downtown Program, as one of only three finalists in the Destination Award category for their *Tourism for Tomorrow Award*. And in 2009, the sixth annual *Survey of Destination Stewardship*, conducted by the National Geographic Society's Center for Sustainable Destinations, ranked Vermont fifth in the world and first in the United States for our stewardship and authenticity.

In all, travel and tourism accounts for 38,000 jobs in Vermont, contributes $1.6 billion in spending and brings 14 million people to the Green Mountains each year. That is why I have been a consistent supporter of this industry. My administration worked hard to strengthen this important economic engine and source of employment. We revitalized our tourism website, www.vermontvacation.com. We strengthened *Vermont Life* magazine by putting it on a sustainable fiscal ground, at a time when many magazines struggled to survive. I supported the state's marketing efforts through my budgets.

We launched a partnership with retail establishments across the state to serve as Info Ambassadors, helping make our state more welcoming to those who want to spend time and money here. In 2009 and 2010, I pushed for additional funds for our Department of Tourism and Marketing so they could work with our partners like the Vermont Ski Areas Association to market our state in the large population centers within a few hours drive from our mountains.

A Special Niche

Vermont has the distinction of being the most desirable domestic domicile for the captive insurance industry in the United States. I was determined to ensure that our standing would, in no way, be diminished. During my eight years as governor, I worked hard to ensure that our position as the "gold standard" domicile for the captive insurance industry was not only maintained – but was enhanced.

The captive insurance industry provides nearly 1,500 good-paying jobs for Vermonters and brings in millions of dollars to the state each year. My administration and the Legislature worked continuously to adjust to the changing needs of the industry. To keep up with emerging trends, we committed each year to ensuring that our statutes reflected changes in the market. Those efforts have paid off. We granted our 900th captive insurance license in late 2010 – up from about 600 in 2003. During the Great Recession, as much of the captive industry retreated, we saw continued growth in Vermont. In fact, a number of off-shore captives re-domiciled to the United States, and many right here to our state.

Exploring Markets Abroad

Economic development is not solely a matter of legislative initiatives. I pursued opportunities to create jobs halfway around the world by seeking investors ready to support Vermont employers and workers. In October 2009, I led a delegation of Vermont business leaders on a mission to Asia to drum up support for the EB-5 Immigrant Investor Program. EB-5 is a federal program that allows foreign investment in exchange for visa preference, if that investment creates jobs. Vermont's EB-5 Regional Center is administered by the Agency of Commerce and Community Development and is the only state-run Regional Center in the country and arguably the most effective.

The 2009 mission, my second visit to Asia as governor, yielded millions in new investments for Vermont companies like Jay Peak Resort, Country Home Products and Seldon Technologies. We also sealed a deal to bring a new biotech firm to the Northeast Kingdom when AnC Bio of South Korea agreed to set up a subsidiary in Newport. I returned to follow up on the success of the 2009

EB-5 mission in 2010. At a time when American businesses were struggling to attract capital, the EB-5 program was helping Vermont businesses overcome that barrier to growth. More than $100 million has already been identified as a result of the program, and many more opportunities remain.

A Relationship Renewed

Pursuing an international economic development agenda does not mean we have to travel far. In fact, Vermont's largest trading partner happens to be our neighbor to the north. By 2010, forty-six percent of our exports go to Canada, roughly $1.1 billion worth of goods. Vermonters sell more goods to Canada than to our next top 11 trading partners combined. Nearly 20,000 jobs in our state can be attributed to this important relationship. Likewise, Vermont attracts $2.5 billion worth of goods from the north. Our tourism economy draws a large number of Canadian visitors as well – nearly 750,000 annually, who spend $141 million throughout our economy.

As our closest Canadian neighbor, there is no question that a healthy and strong relationship with the Province of Quebec is critical for Vermont's economic prosperity. But our relationship is much more. It includes education, trade, energy, the environment, transportation and more. It is a relationship, indeed a friendship, which has its roots in a shared history and culture.

Shortly after I was sworn into office, a transition also took place in Quebec. A new government, led by a new Premier, Jean Charest, took control in April. I asked Lt. Governor Brian Dubie to attend the inauguration in Quebec City with a message that my administration was committed to rebuilding our historic relationship. Later that year, in December, I made my first official visit to Quebec City – the first of at least annual meetings with Premier Charest. Our relationship grew as we worked together on a range of issues from the environment, where we shared an interest in protecting Lake Champlain and Lake Memphremagog, to the evolving challenges at our border.

We also celebrate our history. I traveled to Quebec City to commemorate the 400th anniversary of its founding in 2008. A year later the people of Quebec joined us for the Lake Champlain Quadricentennial – a major undertaking and an important celebration that highlighted the importance of the lake to

Vermont and our economy. With hundreds of events throughout 2009, people from all over the world had the opportunity to visit our state and learn what we have to offer.

The friendship between Premier Charest and me was an important part of my years as governor. Together, we ushered in a golden age of Vermont-Quebec relations, the benefits of which flow directly to the people of both jurisdictions. In March 2010, as a further recognition of the importance of this relationship, I was inducted as an *Officer of l'Ordre national du Quebec*, the Quebec government's highest honor – becoming the first sitting foreign government official to receive such an honor. Later that year I was welcomed into the Society for Distinguished Canadians and Americans by the Maple Leaf Foundation, an organization dedicated to cross-border understanding.

Clean, Affordable, Renewable Energy

The two-day visit to Quebec City in March of 2010 was not just about receiving a cherished recognition from a great friend. Energy, critical to the Vermont/Quebec relationship, was also on the agenda. On March 11, Vermont's two largest utilities, working on behalf of other Vermont utilities, reached an agreement, in principle, for the purchase of clean, renewable power from Hydro-Quebec at a competitive rate for 26 years. Five months later, the agreement was confirmed at a contract signing ceremony in Essex.

Energy is, perhaps, the most recognizable economic benefit we realize from this historic partnership. For the next quarter century the people of Vermont will receive roughly a quarter of our electricity from Hydro-Quebec. The competitive, stable price is critical to the economic success of our state in the coming years. And because that energy is clean and renewable, we will continue our energy leadership, strengthening the Vermont brand and protecting our environment. It is an example of *The Vermont Way* that I spoke of in my first Inaugural Address. That is, environmental gain and economic gain are not mutually exclusive; in fact they are codependent.

This new power agreement is a tremendous step forward and it was enhanced when the Legislature agreed to define large-scale hydropower as renewable, making Vermont the first state in the nation to do so. Vermonters now have the potential to benefit even more than we already will from the power agreement reached by our utilities and Hydro-Quebec.

Fighting Back Against the Great Recession

At the beginning of 2008, a coming economic storm appeared on the horizon. Unemployment began slowly creeping upward nationally, but most Americans could not imagine how deep the economic downturn would become. The Great Recession officially lasted from December 2007 to June 2009. The U.S. unemployment rate would reach double digits for the first time in decades.

As the signs of economic peril grew stronger, I presented a 15-point *Economic Growth Initiative* to Vermonters in April 2008. My proposals included a mortgage assistance program, investments in transportation jobs, job creation tax credits, very low-interest capital for small businesses and startups, investments in downtown development, my New Neighborhoods affordable home construction initiative and a sales tax holiday to boost retailers. I noted that the unusual conditions of the national economy – a sub-prime mortgage crisis, spiking energy costs, and an international credit crunch – require us to take decisive action and urged the Legislature to act swiftly to pass my plan before the end of the legislative session.

The Legislature convened a Special Committee on Economic Recovery and Opportunity to evaluate and act on my proposals. After some debate, they implemented much of what I had requested. But even as the Legislature finished its work in 2008, I told lawmakers that:

> *"Vermont must remain vigilant – we will not rest on our laurels. We must resolve to take whatever steps are necessary to ensure we are the first state to emerge from this economic downturn with a stronger, more innovative economy. We've done it before – most recently in 2003 – and we can do it again."*

As the nation sunk deeper into the recession, we worked swiftly to push back against the tide. I proposed an additional package of initiatives to jumpstart the economy in October 2008. Among them were a research and development tax credit, the development of a statewide Smart Grid, and Opportunity

Zones to encourage the reuse of old industrial facilities. My administration also convened an Economic Response Team to aid struggling businesses and stem layoffs by helping them access information and resources to weather the storm.

In early 2009, shortly after President Barack Obama was sworn into office, I traveled to Washington. My gubernatorial colleagues and I met with the President-elect two months earlier in Philadelphia to talk about how the federal government and state governments could work together in a time of extreme economic distress. During this latter trip I had the opportunity to meet the new president to discuss the need for immediate action to help put Americans back to work. It was an honor to be the first governor to meet with President Obama in the Oval Office.

At the time, I lent my support to the idea of an economic stimulus package, believing that an investment in job-creating programs would be a much needed boost to get people back to work. And as vice-chairman of the National Governors Association (NGA), I fought to ensure that whatever Congress passed would give states enough flexibility to effectively implement one of the largest economic programs in the nation's history. As I worked to protect the interests of states in Washington, I was also taking steps at home to prepare Vermont to make the most of additional federal resources by creating a new Office of Economic Stimulus and Recovery, housed in the Agency of Administration, to oversee the monumental task ahead.

The American Recovery and Reinvestment Act (ARRA) passed in March 2009 and I focused on ensuring that the federal recovery money was used to position Vermont for economic success, especially in the areas of telecommunications, health information technology, and transportation. I knew that for the economic recovery package to be successful, we had to be responsible in how we used federal support. With the influx of federal dollars came an urge to use those one-time funds for on-going expenses as state revenues quickly declined.

I proposed a new package of economic development investments using the flexible funds offered under ARRA. *SmartVermont*, as the initiative was known, directed these funds to Regional Development Corporations, the Center for Emerging Technologies and tourism promotion. Funding would be increased for VEDA to help small businesses and farms access lower-cost capital at a time when capital was difficult to come by. Additional funding would be made available to the successful Vermont Training Program to help workers upgrade their skills.

The Legislature ultimately passed some of my ideas. Funding for a statewide Smart Grid came by way of successful grant applications coordinated by my administration. But the Legislature chose not to allocate all the flexible stimulus money – about $9 million – in 2009 as I had called for with my Smart-Vermont proposal.

As we entered the 2010 legislative session, I renewed my call to invest as much of the federal stimulus money as possible in job-creating programs. By the end of the session, I was pleased to sign an economic development bill, which allocated all the flexible stimulus money for job creation as I had advocated the year before. The jobs bill increased funding for tourism promotion, workforce training, the farm economy, last-mile broadband and small business lending.

◆ ◆ ◆

I am proud of what we accomplished to strengthen Vermont's economy, today and years to come. Vermont secured a large portion of its energy future from clean, renewable and affordable sources. Critical economic development programs, like VEGI, are in place to encourage Vermont employers to expand here and others to locate here. The tourism economy is healthy and becoming more diversified with new agri-tourism ventures flourishing. Vermont businesses have an advantage in attracting foreign investment as a result of the strong focus on the EB-5 program. And the state's reputation for environmental excellence, quality of life and a well-educated workforce make Vermont a desirable place for next generation businesses.

Building a Foundation for Success

"Investments must continue in Vermont's infrastructure that support existing industries and spur economic growth."
— Eighth Budget Message, 2010 —

THE LONG-TERM ECONOMIC success of our state will depend on our ability to secure an infrastructure to support jobs in the next decades of the 21st century. That is why I prioritized investments in our roads and bridges, embarked on an ambitious initiative to bring cell phone and broadband service to every corner of Vermont, and pushed for more funding for higher education and workforce training. We worked to make homes affordable for working families and to keep our downtowns and village centers as vibrant hubs of commerce and community.

Restoring Critical Infrastructure

Protecting and rebuilding the state's transportation infrastructure rarely makes front page news, but in a rural state like Vermont, safe and well-maintained roads and bridges are essential to our economic and social well-being. For years, the state had not made transportation funding the priority that I thought it should be and taxes collected for the purpose of investing in transportation were diverted to pay for other aspects of state government. In 2003, $43.2 million was diverted from the Transportation Fund elsewhere.

Ensuring that funds dedicated to transportation were actually spent on transportation projects was a critical element of increasing the state's investment in and improvement of its infrastructure. I promised to restore funds dedicated for transportation to the Transportation Fund and every year we did starting in fiscal year 2004. By my final budget we had decreased the "raid" by 36 percent from 2004 and had sent nearly $65 million back to the Transportation Fund for its intended purpose.

In addition to more funding, my administration pursued smarter funding choices to make each dollar travel further. The cost of maintaining the state's aging infrastructure increases with time. That, combined with the need to ensure the safety of the traveling public, led me to refocus our transportation priorities with the *Road to Affordability* in 2006. The Road to Affordability made early intervention and preventative maintenance a top priority. But investing in the upkeep of roads, bridges and culverts was not the totality of our approach. By realigning how the Agency of Transportation prioritized its spending, each dollar invested by taxpayers would have a better return on investment.

State government would now optimize its resources by focusing on a small number of significant large projects. Limited resources are no longer spent on unnecessary amenities unrelated to safety and environmental protection. Proposed new roadway projects must explore innovative financing methods to be considered for the Transportation Capital Program. To avoid costly spending on design and redesign of projects not yet certain, a new just-in-time delivery of design was instituted by the Agency. This ensures that design costs are incurred only when there was a reasonable expectation that the project will commence.

In the spring of 2008, after a particularly harsh winter caused significant deterioration of the state's roads, we made an emergency investment in our highways. I instructed the Agency of Transportation to find money above the normal paving budget to resurface some of the worst damaged roads in the state. *Operation Smooth Ride*, as it was known, would contribute to the resurfacing of 80 miles of road – on top of the 270 miles already committed – in 25 towns across the state.

As the economic downturn of 2008 deepened and talk of a federal economic stimulus heated up, I advocated for transportation spending as a central component to any proposal from Washington. On December 11, 2008, I testified before the U.S. House Appropriations Committee about the impact of the recession on state and local budgets. I told the committee, "Investments in ready-to-go infrastructure projects are a cost-effective creator of high-paying jobs. It's estimated that every $1 billion in transportation infrastructure spending generates approximately 35,000 jobs and $5.7 billion in additional economic activity."

When the American Recovery and Reinvestment Act (ARRA) was enacted in March 2009, my administration was already prepared to ensure that Vermont would not waste this opportunity. We received two substantial competitive transportation grants. Six million dollars went to safety improvements at the Knapp Airport in Berlin and the upgrades were completed within a year. Another $52 million was awarded to upgrade passenger rail service by increasing speeds along Amtrak's *Vermonter* line.

In November 2010, I joined our congressional delegation in St. Albans to drive a "golden spike" and officially kick-off that rail stimulus project. Over the long term, this project will greatly improve our passenger rail service as it is designed to dovetail with an additional $110 million in stimulus-funded track improvements in Massachusetts and Connecticut. These improvements will ultimately result in a nearly 90-minute reduction in the time it takes the *Vermonter* to travel from St. Albans to New York City. In the short term, construction of the Vermont portion alone will generate an estimated 150,000 man-hours of labor over two years.

ARRA funds were also put to work achieving the priorities of the Road to Affordability. In the summer of 2009, I targeted $10 million immediately for municipal paving, bridge repair and other transportation enhancements. We were recognized for our speed in deploying stimulus dollars. In total, Vermont received over $137 million, not including the competitive grants for rail and airport improvements, for transportation infrastructure funding.

I also worked to maintain the critical transportation and travel linkages between Vermont and Canada. After September 11th, the security demands at the international border changed forever. In 2004, Congress passed the Intelligence Reform and Terrorism Prevention Act, requiring all travelers to present a valid proof of identity and citizenship when entering the United States as part of the Western Hemisphere Travel Initiative. By July 2009, those crossing the Vermont-Quebec border were required to present a valid form of identification – a departure from the historically easy passage between the neighboring jurisdictions.

To ensure that the historic relationship between Vermont and Quebec would not be impaired by this new and necessary requirement, we set out to find an alternative to the passport requirement. On September 26, 2007, I joined Homeland Security Secretary Michael Chertoff in Burlington to sign a Memorandum of Agreement allowing Vermont to develop an Enhanced Drivers License (EDL). The EDL is an optional driver's license that links to a secure information database verifying citizenship. Vermont became one of only four states to offer the EDL alternative when the first ones were issued in February 2009. Nearly 30,000 have been issued in less than two years. I also encouraged federal officials to accept similar alternatives for Canadians to travel more easily to the United States. Quebec began issuing EDLs in 2009, ensuring a continued expeditious and secure flow of trade across our international border.

For more than two decades, Vermonters have been pursuing a commonsense change for Interstate weight limits in Washington. In 2010, after decades of work in persuading the federal government, I signed a bill increasing weight limits from 80,000 to 100,000 pounds for trucks on the Interstate system after Congress authorized a one year pilot program for Vermont and Maine. The change accomplished multiple goals. It allowed more efficient, affordable and environmentally sound movement of goods across our state. And it relieved town highways from the wear and tear – and safety concerns –of having heavy trucks traveling through downtowns. Unfortunately, by the end of my term Congress had not extended this pilot, and our pursuit of this commonsense policy must continue.

By 2010, with help from the federal stimulus, I signed the largest transportation budget in state history at $585 million. The paving budget – which was $21 million when I took office – grew to a high of $117 million in fiscal year 2010. The budget for bridges – $47 million in fiscal year 2003 – rose to $113 million by the end of my tenure. We increased funding for municipalities through the Town Highway Structures Program and the Class 2 Roads Program. The Town Highway Program saw a 67 percent increase over eight years, and the Class 2 Program grew 70 percent over the same period.

Vermont saw a number of significant transportation projects started and completed during the last eight years. The Missisquoi Bay Bridge was started in

2004 and completed in 2007. One of the busiest sections of Route 7 between Shelburne and Burlington was reconstructed, improving safety and traffic. A reconstruction of Route 7 between Brandon and Pittsford began in 2009. The Western leg of the Bennington Bypass opened in 2004 and the northern segment was well underway by the end of my tenure, with construction expected to be complete by 2012. The Morrisville truck route is expected to begin construction in 2012.

In late 2009, the condition of the historic Champlain Bridge, which connects West Addison, Vermont and Crown Point, New York, was determined to be unfit for travel. The 80 year-old span was a critical social and economic link for those in that region of our state.

Working with New York, we acted quickly to restore travel options between Vermont and New York. Within days we reached an agreement with the Lake Champlain Transportation Company to offer temporary free ferry services. A pedestrian ferry began running, thanks to the generosity of the Basin Harbor Club, and public transit options were made available for individuals on both sides of the lake. We made sure that affected businesses had information about available resources to help them adjust to life without the bridge. In 2010, I worked with the Legislature to appropriate federal stimulus funds to help affected businesses.

On December 28, 2009, I detonated the charges to demolish the old Champlain Bridge and in June 2010 New York Governor David Paterson and I broke ground on the new bridge.

During my tenure, Vermont's transportation infrastructure has seen improvements across the board. The state's roadways and bridges, by every measure, are in better shape than before. The percentage of the Interstate bridges deemed structurally deficient fell from 12.8 percent in 2005 to 6.7 percent in 2010. The percentage of deficient state highway bridges fell from 20 percent in 2005 to 11.2 percent. And the percentage of structurally deficient town highway bridges fell from 17.6 percent to 10.2 percent.

The emphasis on paving resulted in significant improvements to the state system, which in 2008 saw 36 percent of its pavement in very poor condition – dropping to around 30 percent in 2010.

Connecting to the 21st Century Economy

Vermont's success in the new economy is not only tied to the strength of our physical infrastructure, but to our technological infrastructure as well. Our ability to adapt to new industries and new technologies is critical to competing in a rapidly changing economy. Ensuring that every corner of the Green Mountain State has access to broadband and cell phone services is necessary. I convened the Telecommunications Advisory Council to begin developing a statewide telecommunications plan in 2003.

Building on their work, I launched the *e-State Initiative*, with the goal of making Vermont the nation's first true "e-state" by the end of the decade. To facilitate the work, I asked the Legislature to create the Vermont Telecommunications Authority (VTA), as well as to streamline the permitting of the site infrastructure necessary to carry the technology to every Vermont community. The Legislature took up my call and established the VTA, authorizing up to $40 million in revenue bonding authority to finance the work.

But meeting our goal proved challenging, particularly as capital markets around the world collapsed. Funding for the significant upfront costs required was strangled by the Great Recession. Although the private markets struggled, our early preparation put Vermont in a strong position to take advantage of an unforeseen opportunity.

In early 2009, when the federal stimulus package was passed, $7.2 billion was made available for broadband projects across the country. With a telecommunications plan already in place and the VTA working with private providers to coordinate efforts, we were well positioned. My administration worked with the VTA, private providers and others to ensure that Vermont maximized its potential funding.

In June 2009, I traveled to Washington to meet with Vice President Joe Biden and encouraged him to expedite the deployment of technology infrastructure funds. Thanks to the structures we had in place from the e-State Initiative, Vermont was ready to deploy the dollars quickly and effectively.

By the end of 2010, Vermont had received nearly $250 million from ARRA for broadband and Smart Grid build-outs – essentially securing the funding to complete our ambition to become the first true e-state. While the 2010 goal would not be met, Vermont is well on its way to achieving a true 21st century infrastructure to grow, prosper and create jobs.

A Smarter Approach

Just as technology is necessary in the 21st century economy, so too is a strong workforce. Vermont is blessed with highly skilled, highly motivated and highly innovative people – positioning our state to meet the demands of a changing economy. We have among the highest graduation rates in the country and our students consistently perform near the top in education assessments. But for too many the dream of affordable post-secondary education is out of reach.

Our ability to support a vibrant job market is further threatened by the disturbing demographic trends. There is a quiet crisis that, if ignored, will undermine the state's economic security. Between 2000 and 2010, Vermont's population growth was 2.8 percent – the slowest since the Great Depression. As the state with the second oldest median age, it is quite clear that we are struggling to maintain a necessary working population base. If we do not make systemic changes, within a quarter century the number of retirees will double, even as the number of working-age Vermonters continues to shrink. We have the lowest birth rate in the nation. Within the next decade we could see 15 percent fewer Vermonters under the age of 25 than there were a decade ago.

We see these trends clearly in our primary and secondary school populations, where enrollment has dropped from roughly 106,000 students in 1997 to 91,000 in 2010. Some projections foresee enrollment falling below 80,000. Further, Vermont is now experiencing net domestic out-migration and is threatened with a falling state population if trends are not reversed. This disturbing demographic profile makes efforts to retain young Vermonters who are already here, and encourage others to make the Green Mountains their new home, critical to our future economic well-being.

One cause of this challenge is that too many young Vermonters are forced to pursue an education elsewhere – and often they do not return. That is why I pursued an aggressive agenda to make college more affordable and entice young Vermonters to choose a life here after graduation.

We took our first steps in 2003 with the enactment of a new state tax incentive for investors in the Vermont Higher Education Investment Plan -- a credit which we increased over time. Vermonters can receive a state income tax credit for contributions to a college savings account. The tax credit was designed to encourage young families to begin saving for college early.

Although saving for college is important, we can not ignore the ever-increasing costs of higher education. Young Vermonters and their families are simply having too difficult a time affording those costs. That is why I offered a bold approach in my 2006 State of the State address. *Vermont Promise Scholarships* were the centerpiece of my effort to retain our next generation. The plan was to award 12,000 scholarships to Vermonters who attend Vermont colleges and universities over the course of a generation – 1,000 per year.

The University of Vermont, the Vermont State Colleges and the Vermont Student Assistance Corporation (VSAC) would have been able to provide need-based and merit-based scholarships of between 25 and 50 percent of tuition in return for asking graduates to stay in Vermont for at least three years after graduation. The plan, at a cost of $175 million over 15 years, would have been funded largely by money the state was to receive from a legal settlement with tobacco companies.

I regret that the Legislature did not go as far as I had hoped, but they did agree to start down the road of making college more affordable by setting up a Next Generation Commission to report back with recommendations the following year.

On May 23, 2007, many of those recommendations were implemented when the General Assembly passed and I signed H. 433. This scholarship and workforce development bill strengthened the link between employers and Vermonters who sought high-wage and high-skill jobs by providing a new Next Generation scholarship program, more money for workforce training programs – including funding for internships – and an expanded loan forgiveness initiative for Vermonters pursuing health care careers. The *Next Generation Initiative* created a consolidated Workforce Education and Training Fund and strengthened the Vermont Training Program to help employers provide training for employees to upgrade skills and help their companies compete and grow.

In 2007, I was honored to accept the New England Higher Education Merit Award from the New England Board of Higher Education for my efforts to make higher education more accessible and affordable for Vermonters. Ultimately, it is about helping young Vermonters achieve their dreams and the Next Generation Initiative is a key tool in that endeavor.

During my eight years in office, funding for the University of Vermont, Vermont State Colleges and the VSAC saw steady increases. In addition, the Next Generation Initiative contributed millions to preparing Vermonters to compete in the 21st century economy.

Although we made significant strides in prioritizing higher education funding over the past eight years, Vermont still has a long way to go to bring its support to competitive levels. Cultivating a next generation with the skills to lead Vermont into the future also means focusing on our most precious natural resource – our children – earlier in life.

Mentoring is a well-researched approach to helping our next generation make good decisions about their health, improve self-esteem and enhance classroom performance. The benefits do not flow exclusively to our children. Mentors, the adults who give their time to give a young person a better start, gain from what they learn and help build stronger communities in which to live.

The *Vermont Mentors!* initiative was created to enhance community and school-based mentoring programs by redoubling our recruitment efforts. Through the program we are providing technical assistance to those creating mentoring opportunities, as well as funding to help expand mentoring capacity throughout the state.

Ensuring that young Vermonters are getting the best start possible is a goal we all share. Over the years, early child care programs have changed dramatically and so have the demands. Today, two parents working is often the norm. In June 2006, I signed an Executive Order creating the Building Bright Futures Council – a public-private partnership to better integrate Vermont's vast system of services. In 2010, I signed a new Executive Order extending the mission and work of the Council.

We have a strong system of early education in Vermont. That is proven by the success of our children in elementary and high school. But we can always do better to give all young Vermonters a strong head start. Education is a continuum throughout life. However, funding for education is greatly focused on K through 12, at the expense of early and post-secondary education. That is why I proposed rebalancing our support of the education system.

Affordable Homes, Vibrant Downtowns, Healthy Communities

The availability of affordable housing is another challenge we face in keeping young families in Vermont. Even after the precipitous drop in housing prices nationally with the Great Recession, Vermont's median home price was $190,000 in 2009. At that price, a home buyer would need to make $57,000 a year, come up with $15,000 for a down payment and pay closing costs to buy such a home. Although we are thankful that Vermont avoided the depths of the foreclosure crisis experienced in other states – thanks in part to responsible lending and borrowing practices – Vermont continues to have a tight housing market that makes it difficult for young families to achieve the dream of homeownership.

As part of my *Affordability Agenda*, I was committed to expanding the availability of affordable homes. I proposed the *Economic Growth Center* initiative as part of my first budget in 2003. While this effort focused on many aspects of development, one critical element was locating affordable housing units near commercial and retail space. To honor Vermont's historic patterns of growth and prevent sprawl, locating housing near where people work and shop is a commonsense approach.

In 2005, I signed Act 183, creating a "Growth Center" designation that allowed for streamlined permit requirements in approved communities. The first "Growth Center" was approved in Williston in 2007. Since then, Williston has been joined by Bennington, Colchester, Montpelier, Hartford and St. Albans as approved "Growth Centers."

I continued my call for policies that would make housing more affordable for Vermont families. My *New Neighborhoods* initiative aimed to encourage development of housing in downtowns and villages. The proposal provided tax credits for businesses that assist employees with obtaining housing and created a "Virtual Land Bank" program to make donated and surplus state land available for housing. The initiative also called for regulatory reforms to incentivize communities to approve new construction that complemented the existing housing production network.

The Legislature adopted elements of my New Neighborhoods initiative in 2008, providing financial benefits to stimulate new housing development in targeted areas in and around designated downtowns, village centers, new town centers, and growth centers. The Village Square in Essex would become the first "New Neighborhood."

Another key part of my strategy was to continue Vermont's focus on revitalizing our downtowns. I consistently increased tax credits available under the Vermont Downtown Program, an initiative to support the revitalization and rehabilitation of village centers across Vermont. I proposed an *Urban Homesteading* program to encourage the redevelopment and purchase of underutilized space in the upper stories of downtown buildings.

In the late 1990's, the City of Winooski began contemplating the idea of a major downtown renovation. Based on smart growth principles – integrating residential, retail and commercial space – the downtown development was an ambitious undertaking. When I took office in 2003, the project was progressing and the City was looking to secure the necessary funding to move into the development stage. I quickly threw my support behind Winooski's efforts by working to provide the guaranty required to secure a U.S. Department of Housing and Urban Development (HUD) loan for affordable housing in the downtown.

The project was important for a number of reasons. First and foremost, it expanded the availability of affordable housing in the most densely populated region of our state. It helped prevent sprawl by locating housing, jobs, restaurants and shops within a close distance and contributed to good construction jobs during its development stage. The Winooski project provided a shining example to other communities looking to modernize their infrastructure in a way that fits with the character of our state.

My administration pledged Vermont Community Development funds as security for the HUD loan assuming the City could demonstrate an adequate revenue stream to repay the loan. HUD approved a section 108 loan guarantee of up to $24.25 million early in 2004 – the largest such loan of its kind nationally. And on June 7, 2004, we broke ground on the Winooski Downtown Re-development Project. Today, the Winooski Downtown stands as an example of how responsible growth is occurring in our state.

◆ ◆ ◆

Neighborhood revitalization efforts are making downtowns more attractive and affordable. Along with safe communities, those efforts will attract young, working families. We have made unprecedented investments in our transportation infrastructure, improving the quality of our roads and bridges. Increased broadband capabilities are providing for a strong foundation for economic expansion in even the most rural parts of the state. And bringing the dream of higher education within reach of more young Vermonters will allow our state to turn the tide on the disturbing demographic trends now underway. Our state's infrastructure, whether physical, technological or human, must be cultivated and supported.

The Healthiest State

*"Creative ideas can expand access to affordable health care to every
Vermonter; improve quality, comfort, and convenience, while giving
patients and doctors more control over health care decisions."*
— First Inaugural Address, 2003 —

THE RISING COST of health care affects everything from household budgets to
the ability of employers to hire Vermonters and the tax burden. Understanding
that the most important question is not "who pays," but "how much we pay,"
I embarked early in my tenure to bend the cost curve and make health care
more affordable. Better management of chronic conditions, a focus on wellness,
greater implementation of health information technology and a fiscally responsible and patient-centered approach to expanding coverage underscored our
health reform efforts. The innovative reforms we put into place early on became
the model that others, including the federal government, would look to as they
too sought to improve access to health care in America.

At the end of my term, Vermont enjoyed one of the lowest percentages
of uninsured residents of any state. We are well-positioned to adapt to federal
reforms. The expansion of health IT and a patient-centered approach to care
hold promise for reducing costs while increasing quality. Vermont is on the
cutting edge of exciting payment system reforms with the *Blueprint for Health*.
While many of these efforts will take years to bear fruit, many already have begun to blossom. Indeed, Vermont is consistently ranked as the healthiest state
in America – now four years in a row according to the annual *America's Health
Rankings*. All Vermonters can be proud of the national leadership we have demonstrated in this critical social, economic and fiscal challenge – but there will
always be more to do.

A Blueprint for Health

I launched the *Blueprint* in 2003 on the simple premise that health quality and affordability go hand in hand. Calling on private and public institutions to work together to improve the health and well-being of Vermonters while reducing the growth in health spending, the Blueprint encourages healthier lifestyles, better management of chronic conditions, timely and evidenced-based care and the development of more reliable patient information.

Fundamentally, it is working to change the health system from one that treats illness to one that prevents illness and manages wellness by providing information, tools and support for Vermonters with chronic conditions.

In the fall of 2003, I launched the *Chronic Care Initiative*, a key element of the Blueprint. Chronic conditions are the leading cause of illness in the state, and over half of all Vermonters live with a chronic condition. That number grows to nearly nine in 10 for those over 65. In addition to the implications for the well-being of Vermonters, chronic conditions account for more than three-quarters of all health spending in the state. Getting a handle on this significant expense is central to getting control of health costs overall.

Under the Chronic Care Initiative, Vermonters with one or more chronic conditions, like diabetes, arthritis or hypertension, are eligible to participate in the program, which utilizes an integrated team of health and social workers to encourage healthy behaviors and help with related issues such as housing, food security, and transportation to medical appointments. By helping beneficiaries talk with their health care providers, those with chronic conditions are empowered to take control of their situation – avoiding costly medical interventions.

Addressing the high cost of chronic conditions meant not only managing conditions after they developed, but also turning the tide on poor decisions earlier in life that lead to the development of chronic diseases down the road. In 2003, I launched the *Fit and Healthy Kids* program in concert with the Blueprint. Through this program we are combating childhood obesity, encouraging physical activity and healthy eating, and preparing the next generation of Vermonters for a healthier future. As in other health assessments, Vermont has fared well in sustaining a healthy next generation. In 2008, the Every Child Matters Education Fund ranked us first in the nation for overall childhood well-being.

With disturbing national childhood obesity trends, we are always looking to new and innovative ways to keep Vermonters engaged and active, while still having a good time – and taking advantage of what the state has to offer. The *No Child Left Inside Campaign* launched in 2007 is just one example of how state government, through the Vermont State Parks and other partners, can make a contribution. I proudly and actively supported organizations like Girls on the Run, which promote healthy lifestyles for young Vermonters as an important part of the Fit and Healthy Kids initiative.

We funded community efforts through Coordinated Healthy Activity, Motivation & Prevention Programs or CHAMPPs grants. These competitive, multi-year grants have provided support programs ranging from needs assessments in communities around the state to combating lead poisoning in Bellows Falls. In Londonderry and Essex, substance abuse prevention programs were developed; in Woodstock a program encouraged students to walk to school; and in Swanton healthier food options were added to the school snack cart.

A National Model

Encouraging Vermonters to make better decisions about their health is key to reducing growth in health care costs. Reforming the way we pay for care may be equally important. Payment reform is often talked about in theory, but in Vermont we are actually demonstrating how new thinking can really work.

In 2008, the Blueprint took a major step forward as St. Johnsbury, Bennington and Burlington were selected for an innovative pilot effort, utilizing the concept of a Patient Centered Medical Home supported by Community Health Teams (CHT). Combined with enhanced health IT and reporting, health professionals and patients now have an unprecedented level of information to improve care and insurers have incentives to invest in quality.

By 2010, about one-tenth of the state's population was served by the pilots; other than Medicare, all major insurers, including self-insured employee plans, were participating in the fiscal incentives provided under the Blueprint. Most significantly, CHTs in the medical home pilot communities actually receive an enhanced fee for keeping patients healthy, which increases as the providers demonstrate better outcomes.

In 2009, the federal government recognized our successful approach and announced it would allow Medicare to participate in the medical home model on a limited basis. Health and Human Services Secretary Kathleen Sebelius made the announcement at a September 16, 2009 press conference at the White House where she said:

> "Earlier this year, Governor Douglas and several of our fellow colleagues who are governors wrote me in my new position to say, 'We've got a great model, but currently we can do this only with Medicaid, with SCHIP, and with private insurers in our state. We think Medicare should participate in this program. We think there's a real opportunity here to expand to Medicare patients.' And so we took a look at what they were saying and took a look at these impressive results. So today, I'm announcing that Governor Douglas had a great idea."

I was honored to join the Secretary to describe how the innovative *Blueprint* strategy was improving quality and reducing costs at the press conference. In November of 2010, when the federal government announced funding for the Medicare pilot, Vermont was selected as one of eight states to participate. That announcement, along with legislative changes in 2010 that I proposed, will allow for the continued expansion of the Blueprint to more communities and more Vermonters.

Not only was Vermont ranked the "healthiest state" in America for four years in a row – 2007, 2008, 2009 and 2010 – but in March of 2010, I accepted the 2010 *Health Quality Award* from the National Committee for Quality Assurance for our work improving Vermont's health care system through a focus on chronic disease prevention and management resources. The Blueprint has been central to that success. Over time, this strategy will prove to be a major driver of long-term health care cost containment and quality.

Saving Medicaid

When I took office in 2003, the state's Medicaid program faced significant and immediate challenges. As one of the nation's most generous programs with among the highest percentage of its residents on Medicaid, and with health care inflation, the challenge was steep. If actions were not taken that year the program would be insolvent the next year, threatening to leave thousands of the most vulnerable Vermonters without health care coverage. I refused to let that happen, and I challenged the Legislature to join me in saving Medicaid.

On February 20, 2003, a month after I took office, I announced an innovative partnership with Michigan Governor Jennifer Granholm to create the nation's first multi-state purchasing arrangement for pharmaceuticals provided under Medicaid. At the time, Vermont was spending roughly $123 million on pharmaceuticals in the Medicaid program alone and the new collaboration stood to strengthen the state's negotiating position to get a better deal on costly drugs. Our increased purchasing power yielded fast results. By October of 2003, it was estimated that Vermont had cut the growth in the Medicaid pharmacy program by 11 percent.

Throughout my first term, putting Medicaid back on solid footing remained a top priority. However, I recognized that bold and unprecedented changes were necessary if we were going to achieve that goal over the long term.

Global Commitment to Health

To restore the financial integrity of Medicaid, my administration proposed fundamental and pioneering structural changes. Our strategy was comprehensive and forward-thinking, and focused on sharing the obligation of these changes with all parties – participants, providers and government partners. These reforms became known as my *Global Commitment to Health*.

We knew that flexibility from the federal government would allow us to administer our program more cost-effectively by building on the *Blueprint* model of integrated, coordinated care. Focusing on maintaining health is substantially less expensive than treating sickness.

I outlined a concept for a Global Commitment to Health waiver from the federal government while in Washington D.C. for the 2005 National Governors Association winter meeting. I met with U.S. Health and Human Services Secretary Mike Leavitt to sell the plan with a simple concept: Vermont would be provided increased flexibility in its Medicaid program in return for accepting a cap on overall Medicaid spending that was below projections. Under our proposal, total federal expenditures would be locked in and grow at a slower pace than would have otherwise occurred. The enhanced flexibility would allow us to manage the Medicaid program in a way that meets our needs and restores long-term fiscal solvency. Setting Medicaid on a sound fiscal course would also allow us to undertake new initiatives to improve the accessibility and quality of health care.

In June 2005, we achieved a major milestone in Medicaid reform when the federal government granted the state a waiver for our long-term care initiative, Choices for Care. Prior to Choices for Care the only entitlement for Medicaid-eligible individuals was nursing facility care. With the waiver, Medicaid would pay for the setting that is appropriate, whether that be a nursing facility, home-based care or an enhanced residential care home. This not only helped Vermonters in long-term care settings realize a better quality of life by choosing a care setting that made the most sense, it also saved the state considerable resources as caregivers had greater flexibility to provide the kind of coordinated care that is less expensive over time.

In September 2005, the Center for Medicare and Medicaid Services (CMS) approved our more far-reaching waiver. With the Global Commitment to Health waiver in hand, we pursued reforms that we knew would improve quality and save money. Our Medicaid program would become one of the most efficient in the nation, even as it remained one of the most generous.

By 2010, Vermont and the federal government had saved more than $260 million in our Medicaid program. Over the same period, we expanded coverage and programs to more Vermonters and protected the most vulnerable.

The quarter-billion dollar savings was particularly important to preserve the integrity of Medicaid as the Great Recession sent state revenues downward. Vermont's Medicaid program, which was threatened by massive deficits in 2003, remained on solid fiscal ground throughout the historic recession. While other states struggled to meet new federal mandates and run their programs on tighter budgets – sometimes having to put in place draconian measures like dropping non-mandatory populations or instituting waiting lists for new enrollees – Vermont demonstrated that giving a state real flexibility can make a significant difference.

Controlling Costs, Expanding Access

Vermont has experience using its Medicaid waiver authority to expand coverage for the uninsured. Dr. Dynasaur and the Vermont Health Access Plan have expanded coverage to uninsured children and adults. As a result, our uninsured rate has been well below the national average. But still, many Vermonters found themselves in the helpless middle making too much to qualify for help, but too little to afford expensive insurance.

Central to the Global Commitment to Health waiver was flexibility. With increased flexibility we pursued more aggressive health care reforms that expanded coverage to more Vermonters sustainably and responsibly. But even before we received the waivers, I knew we needed to undertake major health care reforms for the fiscal and economic well-being of our state. Reducing the cost of health care and increasing access and quality were key components of my agenda. On September 14, 2004, I outlined my health reform ideas in a speech to the Vermont Chamber of Commerce. My vision for comprehensive health reform in Vermont was built on efforts already underway with the Blueprint.

The reality is that there are no silver bullets – no quick fixes – in solving the health care crisis. Any approach has to be comprehensive by focusing on coverage, quality, cost, and the payment system all at the same time.

My *Prescription for a Healthy Vermont* was a comprehensive plan that included a patient-centered approach by increasing options and choices for consumers. I outlined a number of criteria for health reform, the first being the oldest adage in health care: "First, do no harm." Cost containment had to be a key element, because, at the end of the day, it will not matter which pocket the payment comes out of if we do not address costs – all of our pockets will be empty.

Additionally, patients and doctors need to be in control of health care decisions. Putting people in control also meant increasing health options. Increasing health options meant injecting more choices and competition into our health system to drive down costs. Finally, and importantly, any plan has to be financially sustainable.

Throughout 2005 and 2006, my administration worked with lawmakers, negotiating elements of a health reform package. Finding common ground proved to be difficult. There were honest disagreements between legislators and myself about the shape of reform. By the end of the 2005 session we failed to come to an agreement and I ultimately vetoed a bill passed by the General Assembly. Both sides, however, remained committed to achieving lasting reform and would not give up on finding a bipartisan solution.

That fall I traveled the state, soliciting ideas from Vermonters during a public engagement tour, culminating with a statewide health care summit. Bringing the best ideas back to Montpelier, we once again went to work on achieving real reform. We all agreed that more could and should be done to improve access to health insurance.

Working closely with then Senate President Pro Tem and current U.S. Representative Peter Welch during the 2006 session, we negotiated elements of a package. In May 2006, after a year and a half of working on comprehensive health care reform, we reached an agreement.

The 2006 reforms included more than 60 different initiatives designed to improve access, rein in costs and contribute to a healthier Vermont. The legislation expanded and refocused the Blueprint by allowing insurers to provide healthy lifestyle discounts to those who participate in programs that improve wellness and prevent disease. The legislation made new investments in health information technology. Significantly, the bill created new options for Vermonters to access health insurance. *Catamount Health*, which would begin in the fall of 2007, provided subsidies, based on income, for people to afford private health insurance.

These were extraordinary, even historic, steps toward achieving our goals of providing universal access to affordable health insurance for all Vermonters, improving quality and containing costs, and promoting healthy behavior and disease prevention across the entire lifespan through the Chronic Care Initiative. And we arrived at that point in a way that did not undermine Vermont's long-term economic security.

Our reforms were hailed as an example of bipartisan achievement. As a result of this effort, AARP recognized me as one of "10 extraordinary people who have made the world a better place through their innovative thinking, passion and perseverance," in 2006. "As a Republican governor faced with a solidly Democratic legislature, Governor Jim Douglas could have succumbed to the inevitable gridlock that often mires tough issues," they noted. "But in May, after two years of negotiations, Douglas signed the most progressive health care law in the country, making affordable health insurance available to everyone in the state of Vermont."

Our efforts did not stop with the successes of 2006. In 2008, I signed H.887 and S.283 into law. While not as sweeping as the 2006 legislation, the two bills were significant next steps in improving cost and quality. They increased access to Catamount Health for more Vermonters by relaxing pre-existing condition restrictions and by allowing people with high deductible individual market plans to purchase Catamount Health without having to be uninsured for a year. The 2008 legislation eased conditions on small businesses and enhanced the *Blueprint's* focus on chronic care and prevention. Finally, it encouraged the promotion of health information technology and immunizations.

In 2009, due in large part to the reforms we put in place, the Commonwealth Fund ranked Vermont first on 38 indicators in the areas of access, prevention and treatment quality, avoidable hospital use and costs, healthy lives and equity. The rate of uninsured Vermonters has declined by 25 percent since 2005, even as it has been increasing nationwide.

Healthy Aging

In addition to sweeping legislative reforms, a healthier population requires a strong focus on addressing the specific needs of seniors. As the second oldest state in America, Vermont is in the vanguard of dealing with issues that accompany aging. I worked hard to promote healthy aging and provide the community care options that contribute to that end. Vermont has an active elder population, and giving them the tools to thrive is the least we can do for those who have contributed so much to our communities.

In 2003, when Congress passed the Medicare Prescription Drug Improvement and Modernization Act, it created a new federal prescription drug benefit – Medicare Part D. Despite the expansive new benefit, the enacted legislation created what was known as the "donut hole," where some seniors would be left without prescription assistance for a significant portion of their needs. In response, I ordered the Agency of Human Services to reinstate state benefits for seniors enrolled in Vermont's prescription drug programs prior to the federal changes. While reinstating this "state-only" benefit created significant budget challenges, especially in latter years of my tenure when the economy faltered, I felt it was an important priority and fought for funding year after year.

Like every population, seniors face challenges that require comprehensive and vigilant attention. That is why, in September of 2004, I created a new *Healthy Aging Initiative* and the Commission on Healthy Aging. I tapped Lt. Governor Dubie to lead the commission and charged it with finding ways to utilize resources across the state to promote the well-being of older Vermonters, helping them achieve greater independence and health, while maintaining active lives in their communities. Under Lt. Gov Dubie's leadership, the Commission was instrumental in educating elder Vermonters about changes in health care at the federal level.

Improving Health Technology

A 21st century system of health care benefits from new tools. Electronic medical records are just one example of how we can use technology to both improve care and reduce costs. Timely and accurate patient information can speed a diagnosis or prevent a costly mistake. But adapting these new tools is easier said than done.

In late 2006, I was chosen to lead a national bipartisan alliance charged with promoting and expanding the use of technology in health care. Along with Tennessee Governor Phil Bredesen, I co-chaired the State Alliance for e-Health. The State Alliance – supported by funding from the U.S. Department of Health and Human Services – provides a nationwide forum through which governors, state policymakers and other stakeholders can work together to identify effective health IT policies and best practices and explore solutions to challenges related to the exchange of health information.

Not only did the State Alliance have a strong impact on the national discussion around e-health, but we made great strides in Vermont to increase the utilization of technology in our health care system. I also received recognition from the E-Health Initiative for my efforts to improve health through information technology.

From the very beginning, health IT has been embedded in our reforms. And starting in 2005, the state upped its strong financial commitment to health IT – leading the nation in the highest per capita investment in this critical effort. Those investments included support for the Vermont Information Technology Leaders (VITL), a private non-profit organization, which serves as the coordinator and operator of the statewide, integrated electronic health information exchange infrastructure. Through this public-private partnership, we are breaking down the barriers that have prevented effective health information sharing between and among health care facilities, health care professionals, insurers – both public and private – and, importantly, patients. VITL wrote the first state health IT plan. And, in 2009, I signed legislation to give VITL the responsibility of planning, coordinating and overseeing state health IT policy – mirroring the federal Health Information Technology for Economic and Clinical Health, known as the HITECH Act.

We supported the state's health IT infrastructure by creating a new Health Information Technology Fund in 2008 to pursue initiatives, like those laid out in the State Health Information Technology plan, to increase the use of technology throughout our health care system.

Another important e-health initiative is the Vermont Healthcare Claims Uniform Reporting and Evaluation Systems (VHCURES). VHCURES is using detailed medical and pharmacy claims data to evaluate the effectiveness of our health reform efforts. With this information, which is de-identified and strictly confidential, policymakers and health care professionals can make better decisions to guide future reforms that improve quality and reduce costs.

In 2003, when I took office, Vermont ranked near the bottom in the application of health IT. Barriers stood between providers, hospitals, the state and patients. Tearing down those barriers and helping ensure the technological backbone necessary to expand and safe guard health IT was a top priority. By 2009, our efforts to encourage greater use of technology were widely recognized and Vermont was named the "most improved" for e-prescribing in the nation by Surescripts, a nationwide organization dedicated to the promotion of e-prescribing. I'm very proud that Vermont made enormous strides in the adoption of e-health programs.

National Leadership

In addition to my leadership role at the State Alliance, I was chosen to lead the National Governors Association (NGA) Health and Human Services Committee from 2007 to 2008. After leading the HHS committee, I was elected NGA vice-chairman, serving from 2008 to 2009, when I assumed the year-long chairmanship of the association. Understanding the importance of health reform for state budgets, state economies and the well-being of Americans, I focused my chairmanship on the issue of health care; officially kicking off my NGA chair's initiative, *Rx for Health Reform: Affordable, Accessible, Accountable*, at the National Press Club.

The timing could not have been more appropriate as Congress was beginning a heated debate over federal health reform. That debate would prove not just difficult for Washington, but for states – and governors – who would be responsible for implementing the reforms.

On March 17, 2009, I hosted a Regional White House Forum on Health Reform at the University of Vermont with Massachusetts Governor Deval Patrick. We heard from a broad cross-section of our health care system from throughout New England, including doctors, patients, providers, insurers, policy experts and health care advocates of all kinds – both Democrats and Republicans. It was one of five regional forums to bring a diverse group of people together to discuss concerns and ideas on reforming our health care system.

Despite the efforts of governors, bipartisanship in Washington was in short supply. Believing that we needed to make a change to improve health care at the federal level and that reform would only be successful if there were a broad buy-in, I encouraged a bipartisan approach. I realized that bipartisanship would be the only way our association could have an effective voice in the debate. That is why I worked so hard, throughout 2009 and the beginning of 2010, to bring Republican and Democratic governors together around common principles about the direction of the legislation. Of particular concern were new mandates for states to expand coverage at a time of increasing budget stress. Ensuring that the federal government did not pass a massive unfunded mandate onto states was a battle we fought and one where governors made significant progress.

The debate in Washington, however, was not the impetus of making health care the focus of my NGA initiative. In fact, I had been working on developing it well before there was any thought of a major push for reforming such a significant portion of our economy by the federal government. Further, in 2006, when I was president of the Council of State Governments (CSG), health care was my focus as well. My experiences with reform in Vermont, at CSG, through the State Alliance and the NGA HHS committee made health care a natural fit.

That said, there was no denying the timeliness of the debate in Washington. The initiative aimed at helping states address key challenges in health care by providing governors with the information they need to transition to a new health care system, while preparing states to implement insurance market reforms, state exchanges and other federal mandates. However, Rx for Health Reform was more than working through what was happening in Congress. Helping states develop state-based system improvements and cost containment measures, as we did in Vermont, was equally important. After all, it is states that have led and will lead the way in finding innovative solutions to ever-changing challenges in health care.

In March of 2010, when Congress passed and President Obama signed the Patient Protection and Affordable Care Act into law, I set to work on preparing Vermont to implement the new law. I created a Health Care Cabinet, within state government, to help the state adapt to the changing landscape in health care as a result of the federal legislation. Through NGA, I worked to make sure my colleagues and the states had the tools, resources and information they needed to make the most informed decisions they could about implementing the bill.

◆ ◆ ◆

Health care costs continue to be one of the largest expenses for businesses, families and state government. Addressing rising costs is a struggle that will continue at all levels of government and in the private sector. But Vermont has certainly demonstrated a model that works. From the Blueprint to Global Commitment, we have demonstrated that working smarter in health care does not necessarily mean you have to spend more. As the healthiest state in the nation, we have proven that a serious focus on wellness actually can produce results. And Vermont has demonstrated that bipartisan reform can happen to expand coverage and improve the quality of health care.

I am proud of what we accomplished in health care during my eight years. I am proud of the national leadership I have been able to provide in this arena. And I am proud that we were able to advance reforms outside of the heated political fights that rarely serve the interest of those we serve.

A Safer State

*"When it comes to keeping our neighborhoods safe, there will always
be more to do, but our shared commitment gives me confidence that
we will be ever vigilant. I'm proud that we have worked together to
send a clear message to sexual predators that they will be prosecuted
and severely punished in Vermont... The DETER program has
increased our efforts with better education, prevention, treatment
and rehabilitation for those who suffer from addiction, as well as
strengthened enforcement against drug dealers."*
— Fourth Inaugural Address, 2009 —

VERMONT IS AMONG the safest states in the nation and there is no better place
to raise a family. We are blessed with close-knit communities in every corner
of the state, full of caring people always willing to lend a helping hand to their
neighbors. Vermonters volunteer, sacrifice and do what must be done to ensure
a safer, stronger state. Unfortunately, the Green Mountains are not immune to
tragedy. Drug and alcohol abuse, violent crime and natural disasters have at
times affected the lives of our people with devastating consequences. While Vermont will always have to face new threats to our safety and way of life, I believe
that each of us has the right to feel secure in our homes and towns. That is why
I worked so hard to ensure that Vermonters have the tools they needed to keep
our communities safe and protected.

In the last eight years, Vermont implemented comprehensive drug and substance abuse initiatives, passed sweeping sex offender legislation and combated
domestic violence. We strengthened our law enforcement structures and revitalized our emergency response systems. At the same time we reformed our
corrections system.

A Comprehensive Approach

Like many Vermonters, I knew that drug use and abuse was on the rise. I read the headlines and I heard the stories of how lives young and old were being ruined by these terrible substances and knew that I would have to face this issue with a direct resolve and comprehensive system of programs to address the causes and effects. In addition to experiencing a dramatic increase in the number of Vermonters abusing drugs and alcohol, there was a shift in the substances used by people who were seeking treatment. In the late 1990's and early 2000's the number of Vermonters seeking treatment for heroin dependence increased dramatically. It was clear that our drug programs needed to be reformed to meet these new challenges.

Too many young lives have been ruined by the scourge of drugs and alcohol abuse in our state. One of the first major initiatives I advanced was the *Drug Education, Treatment, Enforcement and Rehabilitation* program, known as *DETER*. The program increased funding for drug counselors in schools and for after-school programs; stiffer penalties for drug dealers, particularly for those who sell to minors and destroy young lives; more funding for proven treatment programs; and an emphasis on rehabilitation in the criminal justice system.

After the program was announced and funded, I set out to establish a single entity capable of coordinating existing resources into a single statewide DETER initiative. It set in motion my plan to assure that every middle school and high school had a drug counselor by 2007. The DETER program drew on federal funding available through the state Department of Education for more after-school programs to keep kids healthy and safe. We emphasized treatment for those addicted by enhancing outpatient treatment and aftercare and with a new 80-bed inpatient treatment facility. We funded residential drug treatment programs and recovery centers across the state. We also invested in offender re-entry programs. It was no longer acceptable to simply lock up those who suffer from drug addiction. Instead, we would focus more resources on the treatment and successful release of these individuals so that they could become productive, successful members of our communities.

The enforcement element of DETER included filling 16 vacancies in the State Police force immediately and another 10 by 2004. We enhanced penalties for those who trafficked, sold or conspired to sell drugs. We created new, undercover Heroin Enforcement Action Teams (HEAT). We enhanced Vermont's drug court system and we encouraged community involvement. Eleven recovery centers, faith-based organizations, Vermont Kids Against Tobacco, and the Governor's Youth Leadership Conference are just a few important examples of organizations across Vermont that are helping Vermonters fight addiction.

The 2003 reforms were just the first step in our fight to protect our communities. I made it a priority to support DETER programs through my budget proposals. I am proud that we placed substance abuse counselors in schools across Vermont, as well as augmented the vast network of programs and services available to those who suffer the disease of addiction. We sent the message to the people of our state; we will not tolerate those who peddle drugs in our communities and if you suffer from drug or alcohol addiction, there is hope.

Protecting our Communities

Ensuring that our sex offender laws are tough, our penalties appropriate and those who pose a continued risk to society are properly monitored was a responsibility I took very seriously.

One of the first commonsense actions we took to make Vermont safer for children was the implementation of an Amber Alert system. It formalized a cooperative program between law enforcement and local broadcasters through legislation in 2003 to send an emergency alert to the public when a child has been abducted and the child's life may be in danger.

In 2004, I called on lawmakers to pass legislation that would reaffirm and strengthen the rights of families all over Vermont to protect their children and neighborhoods. The measure required local law enforcement agencies to notify Vermonters when convicted sex offenders are released into their communities, as well as create an internet registry listing the state's sex offenders. I was proud that legislation passed and was signed into law in 2004 as this marked a first critical step toward giving Vermonters information about the potential dangers in their communities.

Sadly, terrible tragedies continue to impact communities. Although Vermont is a safe place to live and raise a family, we are not insulated from the worst aspects of human nature. That is why I fought hard for the creation of an end-of-sentence review process for dangerous sex offenders to thoroughly analyze the offender's offense history, involvement and progress in sex offender treatment, and mental health status to determine their likelihood of reoffending. I called for civil commitment of those who failed to complete treatment and who meet a legal definition of a sexually violent predator. Unfortunately, the Legislature has not yet acted to impose this important public safety tool.

However, we continued to strengthen our laws in other important ways by imposing indeterminate life sentences to ensure that convicted offenders will be under some type of supervision for the rest of their lives. We established mandatory minimum sentences for serious offenses. And in 2007, I signed legislation to compel incarcerated sexual predators to complete a sex offender program or face more rigorous compliance requirements of an enhanced sex offender registry.

There are few tragedies in recent memory that have had the impact on our state as the horrific murder of a young girl – Brooke Bennett from Randolph. Her brutal death rocked our tiny state and forced all of us in public service to take another important look at how we handle violent sexual predators. Although we had made tremendous strides in making our communities safer there was and will continue to be more to do.

In response, Lt. Governor Dubie launched an effort to gather thousands of petitions encouraging lawmakers to take a hard look at our laws and policies to prevent another tragedy. To redouble our efforts, I proposed a 23-point plan later that summer that was focused on assuring that families, schools, organizations and state agencies are educated and equipped to take all steps possible to protect children; that law enforcement and prosecutors have every available tool for the successful investigation and prosecution of sexual predators; that courts had all relevant information necessary to fashion a sentence that protects the community and enhance sentences for sex offenses; and that convicted sex offenders were aggressively monitored and supervised if released into the community.

Working with the Legislature, we crafted one of the most significant and sweeping bills to strengthen Vermont's response to sexual abuse of children. The legislation was comprehensive, giving government officials tools to address the issue of child sexual abuse in new ways, including increased record checks, new options for prosecution, specialized probation officers, and special investigation units in all regions of the state. It paid particular attention to stopping child sexual abuse before it happens with a focus on public awareness and community involvement. It aimed to equip all those who work in the school system – those who spend perhaps the most time with young Vermonters – with the tools to talk about this insidious problem and identify abuse before it is too late.

In 2009, we strengthened Vermont's internet sex offender registry by expanding the types of offenders and increasing the types of information that must be included on the internet. This was yet another step toward a broader and more informative registry and ensuring law enforcement has important relevant information available during investigations.

It is not just dangerous adults that pose threats to young Vermonters; all too often peers can intimidate one another with tragic consequences. New technologies have the ability to exacerbate an old problem: bullying. On May 18, 2004, I signed legislation establishing bullying prevention procedures for schools. The legislation was prompted by tragedy and I was joined at the bill signing by the father of a young boy who took his own life after being a victim of persistent bullying. John Halligan put it well when he said, "We do not pass laws expecting them to solve problems overnight. We pass laws to make a strong statement of what is expected when we commune as a society. This bill makes a very strong statement of what is expected of our schools when it comes to bullying prevention." One of the greatest legacies of the 2004 legislation was that it raised awareness about the terrible consequences of bullying.

The legislation required the Department of Education to revisit its policies to ensure that students have the ability to report bullying anonymously. It required staff to report bullying to school administrators and that the reports be reviewed or investigated and the information be made available to parents, as well as the development of an intervention strategy to deal with bullying.

But it is not just young Vermonters who are vulnerable to exploitation. Domestic violence must, likewise, be vigilantly addressed. We took important steps to prevent abuse by enacting legislation that extended the authority of a court to issue temporary and permanent relief from abuse orders; criminal-ized violations of orders against stalking or sexual abuse; expanded the scope of domestic crimes; and increased maximum penalties. These steps will empower victims of abuse to get help because they can depend on a strong network to support and protect them.

Corrections

The strain on our corrections system is a challenge we continue to face. Indeed, it is one of the consequences of improving and strengthening the tools we have to make our state safer from drug dealers, sexual predators and other dangerous criminals. Keeping the public – especially the young and vulnerable – safe is the highest priority of government. I am proud that we redoubled our efforts to keep that commitment. I am also proud that as we toughened our penalties and made Vermont an even safer state, we moved ahead with reforms to our system of corrections.

Helping offenders successfully reintegrate into the community, as the vast majority ultimately will, makes our state safer, helps make our population more productive and ultimately saves taxpayers money. In November 2003, I issued an Executive Order creating the Vermont Commission on Corrections Over-crowding to address the rapid growth in our state's prison population. In one decade, the number of people incarcerated in Vermont had doubled and the cost to the state had quadrupled. If the status quo remained, unsustainable spending growth threatened to compromise our ability to provide humane, safe and secure correctional services and facilities.

"This Commission has proposed what we believe to be imaginative and achievable solutions, which if implemented, would have far reaching benefits not only to the corrections system but to the state's General Fund health," the Commission wrote in its report issued during the summer of 2004. Within months my administration began implementing the recommendations. By the end of the year plans were in the works to develop a second prison work camp, double transitional housing, increase substance abuse treatment and job skills development, and launch a pilot project using global positioning systems to monitor the location of offenders in our communities.

I worked with the Legislature in 2005, on a bipartisan basis, to enact reforms to our corrections system. The bill was a thoughtful approach to a very challenging issue. It reduced prison overcrowding by carefully and safely selecting inmates who demonstrate in treatment programs that they are ready for release to the community under tight supervision and control. It held more serious, violent and untreated offenders to mandatory minimum sentences and maximum life sentences so as not to compromise public safety. The bill also required the Department of Corrections to engage in building community partnerships around important issues, such as transitional housing and release procedures.

In addition to those reforms, we included more funding for transitional housing in the budget and began the process of constructing a second work camp through Capital Bill appropriations. We provided methadone as a treatment option for heroin addicts. And the first in-state residential treatment facility for women and adolescents was opened.

Working with the Legislature, we made great strides in reforming corrections. As a result, by 2010, our total incarcerated population is at the lowest point in recent years – falling back to levels of a half decade ago – and we have dramatically slowed the unsustainable budget growth in this critical area.

Safe Travels

During my tenure we not only saw the successful reprioritization of funding for the pavement and construction of transportation infrastructure, but investments to improve the convenience and safety of the traveling public.

We placed digital signs on the Interstate that update motorists about adverse road and weather conditions. The highway safety budget grew from $2.9 million in fiscal year 2003 to $12.2 million in fiscal year 2011. We implemented the state's first Strategic Highway Safety Plan, which brought together a diverse group of safety stakeholders to effectively and efficiently address highway accidents. In addition, programs were developed that work with municipal and regional officials to identify and address areas with crash histories. These efforts continue to reduce crashes and fatalities and result in a safer highway system.

Our Highway Safety Program worked closely with local and county officials to improve highway safety. The "Click It or Ticket" campaign was a highly visible effort to inform Vermonters of the importance of wearing seat belts. And seat belt usage was, indeed, increased – surpassing 85 percent compliance without a primary enforcement law. In 2010, I signed the distracted driver bill into law which increased awareness about the need to stay alert and focused while driving.

Supporting Public Safety Professionals

The policies and legislation that have been enacted during the past eight years are critically important for the safety of our communities. But it is the public safety professionals in our state who carry out the mission every day, at times putting themselves at risk, to keep our communities safe. I have been honored to support these fine men and women however I could.

Providing for the needs of the Vermont State Police was a top budget priority for me every year. When I entered office in 2003, one of my first acts was to present a budget adjustment bill that filled six vacancies in the State Police force. I added funding for another 10 troopers in my first full-year budget and continued to build our force in the coming years. By 2006, I provided funding for all vacant trooper positions.

We continued to strengthen the force, and in 2009, during a time of tight budgets, we, again, added new troopers to the force. In addition, I committed to fully staffing the Special Investigative Units that work with local and county officers to handle some of our toughest crimes.

During my tenure, we opened new police barracks in Derby, Royalton, St. Albans and New Haven. On October 1, 2010, I opened the new 28,000 square-foot forensics laboratory that will provide cutting-edge forensic analysis to help our law enforcement agencies solve crimes for years to come. In 2011, construction will be completed on a new Emergency Operations Center near the lab and the Department of Public Safety's headquarters in Waterbury.

We purchased hundreds of new vehicles to replace an aging fleet, reduce fuel consumption, and improve safety technology. I am proud of our commitment to the Vermont State Police.

I have also been proud to support Vermont's firefighters and first responders. When I took office, the state's fire-related programs were dispersed across different departments, and as a consequence, there was no one office responsible for coordinating those programs and no central point of communications for the fire service and the general public. I worked closely with the Professional Firefighters of Vermont and the Vermont State Firefighters Association and in 2004 I signed the first of many fire service reforms into law, creating the Division of Fire Safety in the Department of Public Safety. Those reforms strengthened and improved our prevention efforts, educating the public about what they can do to prevent fires and stay safe, while building better support for fire departments around the state. In 2005, I signed additional legislation requiring the installation of carbon monoxide detectors in all buildings in which people sleep, at the urging of our fire safety professionals after a fatality on the University of Vermont campus.

As state treasurer, I supported creation of the *Firefighter's Survivor Benefit* that provides financial support to surviving family members of a firefighter who dies in the line of duty. As governor I supported and signed initiatives to ensure that firefighters and their families are protected from the risks associated with keeping our state safe.

In 2009, I broke ground on a new Fire Academy in Pittsford. A year later we opened the new facility at the Robert H. Wood, Jr. Criminal Justice and Fire Service Training Center of Vermont, named in honor of my good friend and a tireless supporter of the fire service. In addition, I supported the new state-of-the-art burn building at Vermont Technical College and the creation of the school's Associates Degree in Fire Science. These new facilities and programs now provide a home for comprehensive firefighter training at all levels of the service.

Emergency Management

Vermont's geography protects us from the worst natural disasters – earthquakes, tsunamis and hurricanes – that have garnered international attention in recent years. That does not, however, insulate us from blizzards, ice storms, floods, wind storms, fires and any number of other emergency events that can befall our state in any season. Being prepared for the unexpected is a responsibility of government.

During my tenure I requested Presidential Disaster Declarations when necessary to ensure that our affected communities got the support they needed to pick up the pieces and rebuild. Communities from St. Johnsbury to Randolph and Barre to Putney have dealt with ravaging fires that destroyed downtown buildings and historic landmarks. And in the aftermath of September 11, every public official had a new understanding of our responsibilities to protect our nation from the unimaginable.

In May 2004, I joined Governor George Pataki and FBI Director Robert Mueller in Albany, New York to announce a new information-sharing pilot program that empowered state and local law enforcement in New York and Vermont to fully participate in countering terrorism and assisting the FBI's Joint Terrorism Task Force. The program provided our nation's first line of defense – our troopers, sheriffs and local police officers – with timely and accurate counter-terrorism information. State and local law enforcement were, for the first time, provided access to more complete information in order to protect the states and communities they serve.

A strong and close partnership with the federal government is essential to an effective emergency response system. Through the Department of Public Safety, Vermont's Homeland Security Unit deployed millions in federal funding to support local communities and first responders. We also made great strides in improving our communication systems between and among various entities responsible for protecting our state and its people.

In September 2004, we undertook an assessment of the wireless communications needs of all public safety and first responder entities within Vermont. By 2005 a more formal structure was developed and the Vermont Communications Board, or VCOMM, was created to manage this enormous task. On June 5, 2006, I issued an Executive Order formalizing the effort. Through the work of VCOMM, we are bringing interoperable communications to Vermont's emergency responders.

Even before the catastrophe of Hurricane Katrina brought emergency preparedness to the front pages, we were hard at work updating our plans to respond to emergencies that might occur here at home. Beginning in early 2004 Vermont's emergency preparedness officials began working with state agencies and non-profit and volunteer organizations involved in emergency preparedness and response to develop an all-hazards preparedness and response plan for the state. The result was a new, 1,000-page plan that significantly strengthened our response and recovery efforts.

During 2009 a concentrated effort was made to catalog existing plans and programs as well as to develop a new emergency operations plan. In April of 2010, Vermont Emergency Management became fully accredited under the national Emergency Management Accreditation Program – a review process for state and local emergency management programs to ensure they are in compliance with national standards. In receiving the accreditation, Vermont had come a long way. In 2004, Vermont underwent an assessment and only met 12 of 54 criteria. Six years later we met each one of the expanded 63 criteria.

Katrina Response

On August 29, 2005, Hurricane Katrina struck the Gulf Coast. It would become the costliest natural disaster in American history, and one of the five deadliest. Vermonters watched in horror as the devastation wrought by Katrina unfolded on the television and I knew that we had to act.

Members of the Vermont National Guard and state emergency and health experts were dispatched to the Gulf Coast to assist in the immediate aftermath. Vermonters across the state were looking for ways to help. Our fellow Americans were sick, hungry, homeless and injured and needed basic essentials like food and water and we could not turn away. For Vermonters looking to contribute to the relief effort, we organized ten collection points around the state, where people could donate basic goods to those whose lives were devastated by the storm. I know that Vermonters are generous, but even I couldn't have imagined the response.

By September 1, Vermonters had filled 35 tractor-trailers with goods headed to Gulfport, Mississippi, among the first to arrive there. But Vermonters were not finished. Operation Special Delivery had two more installments. In all, 65 tractor-trailer trucks with four million pounds of contributions were delivered by Vermonters to those affected by Katrina during the first two weeks of September. More than 525 individuals and businesses volunteered to coordinate the effort, and Vermont mobilized one of the swiftest and most effective relief efforts in the nation. Many Vermonters also opened their homes to those who were left without in the aftermath of Katrina. Offers to shelter people in need that poured in from Vermont families and organizations demonstrated our very best tradition of neighbor helping neighbor.

In a speech to a Special Session of the Mississippi Legislature on September 27, 2005, Governor Haley Barbour spoke about Vermont's efforts in the historical response to this disaster.

> *"....We toured a faith-based feeding station where hundreds of displaced people were eating a hot meal. I met a fellow from Vermont, a truck driver. He and 16 other truck drivers had driven down from Vermont, a small state, very far away, to deliver 17 trailers of food to Gulfport. I couldn't believe it... 17 tractor-trailers all the way from Vermont. Then, he told me it was his third trip."*

This effort is one of the finest examples of the spirit of love and community that exists in our state and I was so proud to lead this effort.

Council of Governors

Hurricane Katrina taught us that not only are people uncommonly good in the face of great adversity, but, unfortunately, our national disaster preparedness systems do not always work effectively. The chains of command can become tangled and hamper the response efforts. To help resolve questions of state and federal jurisdiction, Congress passed the National Guard Empowerment Act of 2007, directing the President to establish a bipartisan Council of Governors – five from each party – to work with defense and homeland security officials on issues regarding the command structure for National Guard and active duty military forces operating within states in response to domestic disasters and emergencies.

In February of 2010, I was appointed by President Obama to co-chair the Council of Governors with Washington Governor Christine Gregoire. Our task was to work with the Secretaries of Defense and Homeland Security, as well as other defense and national security officials, on matters related to the National Guard and civil support missions. Among the most contentious issues was that of unity of effort.

Governors are the Commanders-in-Chief of their National Guards, and those of us on the Council of Governors were committed to protecting that important civilian leadership role. But when federal authorities are necessarily operating within a state's borders we want to ensure that coordination and communication are efficient. Working closely with the Departments of Defense and Homeland Security, governors and the federal government reached a historic agreement to designate dual-hat commanders, with the authority to direct both state and federal forces. The appointment will require the concurrence of a governor and there is an assumption that a National Guardsman would be that dual-hat commander.

As co-chair of the Council of Governors, I am proud of the common ground we were able to find with the federal government on this important domestic response issue. This kind of state-federal effort is unprecedented and I am confident it will greatly improve our nation's response to domestic emergencies and disasters. The work of the Council will continue to find success as a result of our initial efforts. Governors will continue to work on issues ranging from the capacity and equipment needs of our National Guards to preparations to respond to chemical, biological or nuclear events with our federal partners.

◆ ◆ ◆

I am proud that Vermont is one of the safest places in the world to live, work and raise a family. We all have a personal responsibility to help maintain the quality of life we cherish here. And we are indebted to our public safety professionals – our police, firefighters, first responders and our Green Mountain Boys – for their service and dedication to that end.

There will always be threats to our way of life, whether from drugs, criminals, natural disasters or external forces. We are blessed with caring people who are always willing to lend a hand to a neighbor in need. Keeping Vermonters safe and secure is a fundamental charge of state government. It is an ongoing endeavor that must always evolve and adapt. I am proud to have supported these efforts.

The Vermont Way

"Generations of Vermonters have been blessed by a landscape that nourishes the soul... However, the choice we face today is not a choice between jobs or the environment. It is a choice between both or neither. I believe in a third way – The Vermont Way – that recognizes the codependence of our economy and our environment. My administration will work on behalf of each so that we may improve on both."
— First Inaugural Address, 2003 —

MY COMMITMENT TO The Vermont Way formed the basis of my administration's natural resource management, improvement and protection policies. In my eight years, we upheld the environmental traditions of Vermont. We surged to the forefront of energy efficiency and renewable energy policy; secured a green, clean energy future; invested unprecedented resources in the health of Lake Champlain and Vermont's vast network of rivers and streams; promoted alternative forms of transportation, like carpooling and public transit; and took a leadership position in combating climate change through efforts like the Regional Greenhouse Gas Initiative and tough automobile emission standards.

Within state government, I set an example for the rest of the state to follow. We upgraded the state's aging fleet with more fuel-efficient, less costly vehicles. We decreased energy use in state buildings by establishing commonsense policies on heating and air conditioning – saving money as well. And we championed renewable energy in state buildings.

Protecting our Air

Although Vermont has the best air quality in New England, threats from outside our borders are persistent and vigilance is required. There was no clearer example than when International Paper (IP) in Ticonderoga, New York proposed to burn tires as a means of generating energy. While recognizing the economic importance of IP – Vermonters, as well as New Yorkers, are employed there – I proudly joined with thousands of other Vermonters in opposing their plan to burn old tires as an energy source, especially in light of IP's persistent refusal to upgrade the pollution controls at the Ticonderoga facility.

IP maintained that burning processed waste tires is critical to their future viability, as it will provide a significant source of low-cost energy for the plant. IP also asserted that the cost of cleaner technology was prohibitively expensive for the Ticonderoga facility. In my view, those were not convincing arguments and would not ignore the impacts that burning tires would have on air quality in Vermont, especially in Addison County directly across Lake Champlain from Ticonderoga.

Over the years, Vermont has vigorously fought pollution traveling into our region from Midwestern smoke stacks; to allow a new source of pollution to arise so close to our border was unacceptable. We explored all available options, including legal challenges to IP's underlying air quality permit. In the end, our leadership prevailed and IP was compelled to abandon their plan to burn tires without the proper pollution control mechanisms in place. It was a resounding victory for the people, and the environment, of our state.

Combating Climate Change

Our environmental protection efforts have extended far beyond the protection of Vermont's air and waterways. I was proud to continue the Green Mountain State's legacy of environmental leadership by propelling our state to the forefront of regional, national and international efforts to combat climate change.

In 2003, I issued an Executive Order creating the Climate Neutral Working Group tasked with coordinating, documenting and encouraging efforts to meet Vermont's greenhouse gas reduction goals. Much of the work we achieved in this area is the product of this initial effort.

I presented the state's first-ever comprehensive environmental impact and resources management plan in 2004 – setting a goal of reducing government's emissions by 25 percent by 2012. And in 2005, I created the Governor's Commission on Climate Change to take a much more comprehensive look at the impact of climate change on Vermont, including its impact on public health, natural resources and the economy.

As a rural state, nearly half of all of Vermont's greenhouse gas emissions come from transportation. At my direction, in 2005 Vermont signed onto California's updated strict vehicle emissions standards – we were the first state to do so – under section 177 of the Clean Air Act. The Legislature, at my recommendation, codified those standards in state law. The federal government, however, fought the action of Vermont, California and 11 other states seeking these higher vehicle emission standards. In 2007, the Environmental Protection Agency (EPA) denied the waiver required to implement the new standards and the automobile manufacturers sued us in federal court to prevent these standards from taking effect.

By November 2007, with the federal government dragging its feet, Vermont joined California in suing EPA to grant the waiver. As the battle to implement stricter automobile emissions standards waged on, I testified before Congress on January 24, 2008, telling the panel: "Global warming is a complicated problem that will not be solved by any one action. Coordinated state efforts to reduce emissions from the transportation sector should be applauded and the statutory provisions authorizing these state actions must be upheld."

The EPA, yet again, denied our waiver to implement the California standards later that year. But we refused to give in and continued to fight by joining a new, multi-state lawsuit, this time to compel EPA to rule on whether greenhouse gas emissions endanger public health or welfare.

As the federal government continued to stand in the way of Vermont's efforts, I worked to expand support among my colleagues. In May 2009, the Obama administration announced an agreement that paved the way for Vermont to implement and enforce the California emissions standards. Four years after Vermont first signed onto the higher standards, we finally could move forward. As the first state to adopt California's greenhouse gas emissions standards and to successfully defend them against legal challenges by the automobile industry in federal court, Vermont helped to pave the way for this decision – a significant win for the environment.

Groundbreaking Regional Initiatives

Vermont's environmental leadership was on display when I became the first governor to sign on to a groundbreaking regional effort to reduce carbon emissions from power plants.

In remarks to government representatives from around the world in December 2005 in Montreal at the Leaders Summit during the Eleventh Session of the Conference of the Parties to the UN Framework Convention on Climate Change, I noted that Vermont would be the first state to sign onto the *Regional Greenhouse Gas Initiative (RGGI)*. I was the only American governor to attend this global dialogue.

RGGI addresses carbon dioxide emissions from electrical generating facilities in the Northeast. Participating states agreed – beginning in 2009 – to cap emissions from power plants for six years, until 2015. Then, from 2015 to 2019, the states will incrementally reduce emissions by 10 percent. As the first governor to sign on, I ensured Vermont would be instrumental in crafting the framework for cutting emissions and trading allowances.

In 2006, the Legislature formally committed Vermont to RGGI and in September of 2008 the first RGGI auction was held. By that time 10 northeastern states were participating in the program, and other states and Canadian provinces were observing it. RGGI not only demonstrated that governments and the private sector can work together to reduce emissions, but in its first years it netted millions for investment in energy efficiency efforts.

Our regional climate change initiatives extended beyond RGGI. Working through the New England Governors and Eastern Canadian Premiers Conference, Vermont committed to the organization's Climate Change Action Plan, which calls for a 10 percent reduction from 1990 levels in greenhouse gas emissions in the region by 2020. We became a charter member of the Climate Registry on May 8, 2007. And in 2010, we again joined with our regional partners by signing onto an effort to develop a Low Carbon Fuel Standard.

Exporting Vermont's environmental ethic – a matter of both economic and environmental imperative – was the focus of my first trade mission to Asia in 2007, where I met with the Mayor of Shanghai, China to promote clean air, clean water and the fight against climate change. I spoke at the opening of the international Environmental Exposition in Beijing on the same mission – taking the opportunity to promote our state's many products and services.

Toward a Renewable Future

The economic and environmental advantages of "The Vermont Way" drove our emphasis on responsibly expanding the scope of Vermont's renewable energy portfolio. Renewable energy projects have flourished in the last eight years throughout our state.

In 2003, we created a solar and Vermont-scale wind incentive program. Utilizing funds from the petroleum violation escrow fund, we provide financial incentives for hundreds of solar electric, solar hot water and Vermont-scale wind systems. A particular emphasis was placed on defraying the cost of solar energy systems for low-income and multi-family housing units.

I signed legislation creating the Clean Energy Development Fund to promote the development and deployment of cost-effective and environmentally sustainable electric power resources for the long-term benefit of electric consumers in 2005. The next year, I proposed giving municipal renewable energy projects funding from the Clean Energy Development Fund to encourage municipalities to pool their net-metered buildings and sell excess renewable energy back to the grid. This mechanism had the benefit of diversifying our energy portfolio while helping communities put downward pressure on rising property taxes. I supported "green pricing" legislation that provides utility companies with the flexibility they needed to offer consumers specially priced energy from renewable sources.

As world demand for fossil fuels continues to increase, and as prices continue to rise, Vermonters are looking for innovative ways to save money and limit exposure to these volatile markets. In 2007, I was pleased to sign the Energy Efficiency and Affordability Act, a bipartisan effort to invest $4 million in a new all-fuels efficiency program to coordinate expertise, technical assistance and resources, helping Vermonters make their homes and businesses more energy efficient. The funding came from existing revenue sources, including proceeds from RGGI. Vermont is widely recognized as a national leader in energy efficiency investments.

Vermont's environmental and economic future is intricately linked with its energy future. The expansion of in-state renewable resources will be an important source of jobs and clean energy. During my tenure state government made a historic commitment to expanding small-scale energy generation in-state. From the forest products industry where biomass is creating jobs to farms where methane digesters are proving to add value to operations, energy is critical to securing a more economically secure and prosperous future. And in recent years, innovative Vermonters have begun producing electricity from landfills in Moretown and Coventry.

But my energy strategy was also more broadly focused. I summed up my approach in a meeting with President Obama in 2009: "As Washington debates our national energy policy, Vermont's lessons and achievements must be part of that dialogue. From in-state efficiency measures to our regional partnerships, like the Regional Greenhouse Gas Initiative, Vermont is confronting the challenges of energy independence and climate change on many fronts."

As in so many other areas, states are incredibly diverse when it comes to their energy opportunities. If our ultimate goal is to reduce the amount of carbon we send into the atmosphere, then we should not discriminate against certain alternatives to achieve that goal. Rather than a top-down energy policy that favors certain forms of energy over others, each state should be allowed to pursue innovative alternatives that work best for them.

Vermont's example is instructive. By the end of my tenure, we had assembled the greenest energy portfolio in the nation – and one of the greenest in the world – in an economically responsible way. Two-thirds of Vermont's baseload power comes from non-carbon emitting sources.

And with the agreement with Hydro-Quebec and the designation of large-scale hydro as renewable in Vermont, we will continue to receive a significant portion of our energy portfolio from a green, renewable, affordable and friendly source.

Pursuing renewable, carbon-free sources of energy, whether large-scale or small-scale, will be critical in protecting our environment and advancing our economy. As we transition from an economy based on fossil fuels, we will have to be open to forms of renewable energy generation that can power new technologies, like electric cars. And we will need an infrastructure to support this transition.

By the end of my tenure, the future of Vermont's nuclear power plant is uncertain. The need for clean, affordable base-load power is essential in our state. Losing such an important piece of our energy portfolio will leave an enormous void, drive up costs and likely be replaced by dirtier forms of energy. But safety is always paramount. I do believe this plant can be part of our energy future once its safety has been assured, and Vermonters' confidence in its leadership restored.

Building on the foundation set by our pioneering e-State initiative, Vermont was poised to become a leader in smart grid technologies and capture millions in federal funding to build out a statewide smart grid that gives Vermonters more information about their energy usage, and allows individuals and businesses to enhance efficiency efforts, reduce peak energy consumption and pursue more renewable alternatives.

In the fall of 2009, the U.S. Department of Energy awarded Vermont nearly $70 million to help transition to new, environmentally-friendly Smart Grid technologies. This funding is matched by an equivalent investment by Vermont utilities. In addition to the immediate benefits of consumers having more information, this build-out positions Vermont to capitalize on new and emerging technologies, like electric cars and represents another example of our innovation.

Clean and Clear Waters

Clean air and clean energy are vital to our environmental stewardship. So is protecting the precious natural resources that distinguish our state as the best place in all seasons. Vermont's natural gifts, its lakes, mountains, forests and wildlife, make the Green Mountains a special place. They define who we are and support our traditional ways of life. Protecting those gifts is the responsibility of every generation and one that I took seriously.

In my first term, I embarked on "a new commitment to improving and protecting the Lake Champlain basin and waterways throughout Vermont." The *Clean and Clear Action Plan* was launched in September 2003 and it is one of the policy initiatives of which I am most proud. Improving the health of Lake Champlain and Vermont's waterways is a complex task that involves bringing together various groups – from farmers to environmentalists, from developers to sportsmen, as well as working across state and international lines.

Early in 2003, I recall fondly joining my friend, Governor George Pataki, to recommit Vermont and New York to a collaborative effort to fight pollution in Lake Champlain by signing an updated *Opportunities for Action* plan. In 2010, I would again approve a newly updated document, upholding Vermonters' commitment to working with our neighbors to improve the quality of this tremendous resource.

The Clean and Clear program focus was to reduce phosphorous pollution in Vermont's waterways. That effort meant targeting the sources of phosphorous flows. That meant working with farmers, developers and communities to implement best practices, like installing necessary barnyard structures to prevent discharges, minimizing loss of floodplain function, reducing stormwater erosion in urban, suburban and back road settings and eliminating discharges of improperly and untreated sewage.

The Clean and Clear program has supported hundreds of water quality programs throughout Vermont from securing river corridor easements along the Batten Kill and the Missisquoi to providing incentives for planting thousands of acres of cover crops and providing assistance to towns to reduce road-related erosion.

We invested more than $50 million in state funds to support the Clean and Clear program, leveraging over $50 million more in federal funds. As a result, for the first time, a recent analysis of phosphorous flows into Lake Champlain actually showed a decrease.

Together, we have made the state's most significant investment in water quality and set the state on a path to restoring the long-term health of the Lake Champlain watershed. The challenge, however, is one that is thousands of years in the making and will require a sustained effort to avoid sliding back.

Fish and Wildlife

Clean and Clear is not just about improving water quality – it is also about protecting the vital eco-systems of our state. But our efforts extended well beyond the shore's edge. I made restoration of our fish and wildlife populations – and steady, scientifically based management of these resources – a high priority.

Sea lamprey control had been discontinued following an experimental program during the previous administration. By the time I was sworn in, nearly every lake trout and salmon coming out of Lake Champlain had one or more sea lamprey wounds, which had also become more common on other species of fish in Lake Champlain. The lake trout and salmon fisheries in the lake, and the ecological and economic advantages they produce, had all but collapsed. Anglers and other lake enthusiasts were angry – and they had every right to be. At my direction, sea lamprey control was re-established.

Overcoming significant permitting hurdles, including state purchase of an activated carbon slurry filter system to protect the Burlington drinking water supply, the control program was successfully implemented. The positive impacts on the lake trout and salmon fishery have been remarkable. Sampling in 2010 indicated that the cooperative sea lamprey control program, including Vermont, New York and the U.S. Fish and Wildlife Service, achieved the target wounding rate for salmon. The program resulted in significant improvements in the size and number of lake trout and salmon being harvested from Lake Champlain. This has helped buffer Vermont from declines in license sales experienced in nearby states and improved the overall quality of the lake.

Through my capital appropriations, we invested in our fisheries by upgrading and expanding hatcheries. Our walleye population is a particular success to note. Working with groups like the Lake Champlain Walleye Association, Vermonters collected 3.1 million walleye eggs and stocked 200,000 fry, 50,000 advanced fry and over 95,000 fingerlings into Vermont waters in 2009, contributing to the health of our fisheries.

Sporting events like the annual Lake Champlain International Father's Day fishing derby continue to grow as anglers from all over learn about the opportunities for a big catch in Vermont. Because our fish are larger and healthier, we have seen license sales increase. We welcomed New York anglers to our waters, our shores and, of course, our stores, when we agreed to allow for reciprocal licenses on both sides of Lake Champlain.

White-tailed deer management has historically been very controversial in Vermont, but better management of all big game species – deer, moose, bear and wild turkey – was a priority I established in my first campaign. Management of big game species requires a data-driven system for the purpose of determining annual changes in regulation needed to provide for the appropriate harvest of these animals.

During the past eight years, the Department Fish and Wildlife has greatly enhanced technological and statistical abilities for collection and analysis of the data necessary to determine management actions and inform the regulatory process. The result has been striking improvements in harvest opportunities for all four big game species. Comments received from deer hunters were increasingly favorable as a result of greater numbers of older bucks being harvested.

In the eight years of my administration, developing a systematic process and guidance documents to efficiently and effectively direct the process by which Vermont seeks to restore threatened and endangered species was also a priority. A recovery planning process and procedures for operation of the Endangered Species Committee were implemented and it has proven effective.

Following establishment of a template for recovery plans, the "Spiny Softshell Turtle Recovery Plan" was completed and approved. A "Bald Eagle Recovery Plan" was completed. A recovery plan for spruce grouse was substantially complete. Plans for grassland birds and the eastern timber rattlesnake were also underway. We celebrated the success of these efforts when the osprey, peregrine falcon, and common loon were officially removed from the endangered species list.

Among many other achievements in this area, my administration also developed an online licensing system to boost license sales; expedite the planning process for, and active management of, Wildlife Management Areas that provide more public land for wildlife-based activities like hunting, fishing and trapping; completed significant upgrades at our summer Conservation Camps for young Vermonters; and made the deployment of state-of-the-art science and technology a higher priority within the Department.

Forests, Parks and Recreation

We prioritized the active management of state forest land and revitalization of Vermont's state park system during the eight years of my administration. The Department of Forests, Parks and Recreation embraced an entrepreneurial approach to problem-solving in government that reduced its reliance on General

Fund taxpayer-financed spending by more than 30 percent – more than $2 million – while increasing its productivity. Stewardship timber sales conducted by private loggers increased 28 percent. More than 1,300 cords of fuel wood was made available to low-income Vermonters in 2009, including 900 cords from the "cut your own" roadside lot program; and the number of sites on state land available to maple sugar producers more than doubled.

To further reduce reliance on taxpayers, we worked hard to increase park attendance. We expanded use of internet-based communications tools; revitalized our web site; created customer-centric online purchasing and reservation tools; and added innovative new programs like *Check Out the Parks* library passes, which allows Vermonters to borrow a park pass the same way you borrow a library book. We embarked on a record-setting $8.1 million capital construction program that is creating hundreds of private sector construction jobs across the state, revitalizing the park system and improving the guest experience. In the last two summers of my administration, park visits and local economic activity increased nearly 25 percent.

◆ ◆ ◆

Vermont is known the world over for its green ethic. In fact, *Forbes Magazine* named Vermont the "greenest" state in America in 2007. We were also recognized as the "greenest state" in 2009, this time by the *Earthsense Eco-Insights Survey*. In December, 2010 the website *24/7 Wall St* ranked Vermont as the greenest state in American when energy consumption, pollution problems and state energy policies are evaluated. Our state's energy portfolio is arguably the greenest in the nation, and among the greenest in the world. I was honored to be named one of the top ten Green Governors by the *Greenopia* website.

Threats to our natural environment come from far and wide. The challenges, at times, seem too daunting for a small state like ours to confront on our own. But although we are a small state, we can have a tremendous impact. People look to Vermont for ideas and leadership. They look to us to chart a prudent course of environmental protection. I am proud that we demonstrated that leadership. It is a testament to our people, our Yankee ethic and our concern for the next generation.

Fiscal Leadership

"I developed this budget on a set of principles from which I will not stray: First, government must live within its means because every dollar we spend beyond our capacity to pay is a dollar that must be repaid by our children. Second, government will fulfill its commitment to the neediest Vermonters because a society is judged by how it treats the most vulnerable. Third, we should not dip even further into the pockets of struggling taxpayers. Fourth, sacrifice must be shared broadly so that no one is asked to carry an undue burden. Finally, the most direct route back to prosperity is to invest in Vermonters' education, skills and aspirations. My budget lives up to these principles and any budget that arrives on my desk for signature must as well."
— First Budget Message, 2003 —

THE STATE BUDGET is the primary policy document offered by the Administration and debated by the Legislature. It is one of the most important pieces of legislation passed every year. The budget in any form – whether proposed, amended, passed, rescinded, or adjusted – is a running ledger of our priorities. It is axiomatic that there is never enough money for all of the needs of government. Even in boom years, when tax revenue is flowing, there is pressure to fund some programs more and others less, or to raise additional revenue to support new initiatives. In the lean years, these challenges are made much more complex because Vermonters have a greater need for services with a diminished capacity to afford the taxes that fund them.

Despite being the only state without a mandated balanced budget provision, Vermont has a long tradition of crafting responsible budgets. I have been proud to submit a balanced budget each year of my tenure. While folks can

– and do – argue whether budgets are responsible or sustainable, there is no argument about whether they have been balanced. This has been no small feat in the last few years.

Moreover, in each of my budget proposals, I checked base spending growth to stay within inflationary limits. Government must not grow more than the paychecks of working Vermonters.

More Efficient Government

As with any institution, the operations of government can always be improved. Indeed, governmental structures that have developed over time are generally not the most efficient or effective. As circumstances change, government too must evolve.

To ensure that state government was equipped to adapt to new and changing technologies, I created the Department of Information and Innovation (DII) in 2003 to provide direction and oversight for all activities directly related to information technology within state government, including telecommunications services, information technology equipment, software, accessibility, and networks in state government.

That same year, I commissioned a group of leading Vermonters to look at ways we could make state government more efficient. The Vermont Institute for Government Effectiveness (VIGE) pointed to enhanced opportunities for e-government, information technology reorganization and a transformation in the state workforce to improve the workings of state government.

We implemented many of the recommendations through the Strategic Enterprise Initiative (SEI) starting in 2006. We have made great strides in utilizing technology to benefit both taxpayers and those who depend on services. The Vermont Information Consortium (VIC), state government's web portal vendor, was recognized as one of the ten best government portals and websites in the nation by e.Republic's Center for Digital Government in 2009 and 2010.

At the Department of Motor Vehicles (DMV) the modernization efforts include kiosk services and online registration renewals. No longer do Vermonters have to travel to the DMV for routine services, but rather take care of those services online when it is convenient. And we are bringing more services online.

In 2010, my administration launched the *MyVermont* web portal to make it easier for Vermonters to access services across state government, from human service benefits to grant opportunities for small businesses.

Efforts to make state government more responsive were not merely confined to these. We reorganized certain agencies and departments to make them more reflective of their mission. The Department of Labor and Industry and the Department of Employment and Training were consolidated into a single Department of Labor in 2005. The Department of Economic Development and the Department of Housing and Community Affairs, both within the Agency of Commerce and Community Development, became a single Department of Housing, Economic and Community Affairs in 2009. We also consolidated the human resource functions to provide for more streamlined management of state government personnel.

During my first session in the Legislature in the early 1970s, I presented a constitutional amendment that set the stage for a reorganization of our judiciary system. Nearly four decades later I signed into law a sweeping reorganization of the judiciary. Significantly, the bill, H.470, unified the superior, district, family and environmental courts into one superior court with civil, criminal, family and environmental divisions. The 2010 reforms were made possible by the efforts of Chief Justice Paul Reiber. Providing equal access to justice is a fundamental right in our society and no Vermonter should ever be denied that right for lack of resources. Reorganizing the judiciary was a necessary step to ensure that our court system is sustainable and affordable.

During the 2009 session, the Legislature and my administration began the process of looking deeply within the structures of state government to find opportunities for savings that would help us meet the need to adjust expenditures to the reality of falling revenues. I convened *Tiger Teams* of state employees to examine potential savings throughout the budget. The Legislature started working with a consultant on a project that would become *Challenges for Change*. Together, in the 2010 legislative session, we started down the path of Challenges to achieve long-term savings through efficiencies in government, implementing a number of the Tiger Team recommendations, as well as refocusing the way we budget on achieving outcomes.

Fiscal Health and Strength

The structures of government are important. But without prudent financial management no amount of rearranging would improve the operation of programs and services. I learned first-hand the tremendous importance of strong and steady financial leadership by working closely with Governor Richard Snelling and during my many years in state government. I needed these skills when I started as state treasurer in 1995. Vermont had suffered from weak bond ratings that were the fallout of the fiscal crisis in the late 1980's and early 1990's. The weak ratings were a signal from investors that the state had not been living within its means. The slow path back to high marks took many years and many steps. As Treasurer, I worked in partnership with Governor Howard Dean; and as Governor Dean's successor, I worked closely with Treasurer Jeb Spaulding to rebuild the state's credit rating to the best in New England.

In 2007, we were pleased to announce the much-anticipated news: a triple A rating from Moody's, which placed Vermont in the highest tier with other well-run states. Moody's credited Vermont's history of financial management and our manageable debt profile as among the key factors in the decision. Our Aaa/AAA ratings from Moody's/Fitch are significant achievements of my tenure as both treasurer and governor.

We added to that honor in 2010 with an announcement from a website, *24/7 Wall St.* that ranked Vermont as the 4th best-run state in the nation. We have worked to develop a level of excellence in the Administration's financial management.

Although the work of financial accounting, internal controls, and yearly audits is not glamorous, it is the bricks and mortar of day-to-day government operations. When I took office in 2003, state government had not completed its annual audit from 2002 due to the migration to a new accounting system, which had led to a host of problems across the enterprise. This was a key priority in the early years of my governorship. The clean-up work took time and diligence, but it paid off. In 2009, Vermont was awarded the *Certificate of Achievement for Excellence in Financial Reporting* – the highest recognition in the area of government accounting and financial reporting – from the Government Finance Officers Association of the United States and Canada (GFOA) for the

2008 Comprehensive Audited Financial Report (CAFR). This achievement was matched by a repeat performance for the 2009 CAFR.

Keeping our stabilization reserves – the "rainy day funds" – full has been a hallmark of our financial leadership. Although these reserves are sometimes considered a piggybank for additional appropriations, they serve a vital role in stable financial operations by allowing the state to meet obligations without unnecessary short term borrowing. In my first full-year budget, we worked quickly to rebuild the funds after they were drawn on during the brief economic downturn of 2001. Once replenished, we kept the reserves full, despite many calls to use this one-time money to fund ongoing programs affected by budget cutbacks. Looking forward, when revenues rebound, the state should consider increasing the stabilization reserves to provide a bigger cushion during lean budget cycles.

Protecting the Most Vulnerable

The Vermont community has long prided itself on taking care of neighbors in need. The state programs that sprouted over time to support the vulnerable and neediest among us are an offshoot of Vermonters' inherent generosity. From Dr. Dynasaur to Women First, from General Assistance to Green Mountain Care, the range and scope of Vermont's human service and health care programs are remarkable. Vermont's safety net is broad, deep and very secure. We have much to be proud of.

Indeed, in 2009 the *New York Times* rated the scope and strength of the safety-nets of all 50 states. It was no surprise that Vermont's social safety net was the strongest overall. When it comes to my support for our social safety net, the numbers speak for themselves. During the last eight years, the human services budget has increased by 65 percent – a 6.5 percent annual growth rate. Even as the Great Recession ravaged state revenues, we continued to increase our support for those most in need.

While these services are a blessing for those who need help, the fiscal challenge to fund these initiatives is perennial because of ever-expanding populations of need coupled with rising costs for care. The fact is that we cannot protect programs and services for the most vulnerable Vermonters if we allow them to grow unrestrained to the point where they collapse under their own weight. Further, unchecked growth will invariably eat into other areas of state government and shortchange critical items like public safety and environmental protection. It is because Vermont is so progressive in the area of health care and human services that we must remain vigilant and ready to innovate to safeguard our progress.

Over the years, some have criticized any effort to make these programs fiscally sustainable as unconscionable budget cuts. I recall that when we proposed Global Commitment, many proclaimed it would lead to the unraveling of signature programs and loss of care. In fact, the opposite has been true: Global Commitment has allowed us to responsibly expand our health care efforts and make Medicaid more sustainable. I appreciate the commitment of legislative leaders on both sides of the aisle who stood with me to enact these critical reforms.

We live in a region of the country where the ability to heat your home is vital. As the price of oil skyrocketed in 2008, I initiated the *Fuel and Food Partnership*, a collaboration of public and private partners charged with marshaling every available resource to help Vermonters address the rising cost of fuel and food. We made a budgetary commitment to ensure that Vermonters would not have to choose between heating their home and putting food on the table for lack of resources.

It was not just when the price of oil was high that I fought to keep low-income Vermonters warm during the winter months. I was a consistent supporter of the Low-Income Home Energy Assistance Program (LIHEAP), often urging the federal government to live up to its commitment in this critical area.

We addressed an issue within LIHEAP and other state programs that worked against those looking to move from state assistance to self-sufficiency. In 2009, I hosted a Summit on Pathways to Economic Stability, which brought together human service leaders to address poverty. Among the key recommendations from that discussion was that more needed to be done to smooth out the benefits cliff. The benefits cliff – when a small increase in income leads to the termination of services – is often cited as a major impediment for those trying to get back on their feet after falling on difficult times. Within LIHEAP, we changed the benefit structure, expanding coverage to more Vermonters by graduating the subsidy based on income.

We made similar changes in our 3Squares program, formerly known as "food stamps." Again, by expanding eligibility, we are avoiding the situation where individuals are discouraged from finding work. We increased child care subsidies by adding $5 million to the program in recent years so that working families, mothers in particular, would not be forced to forgo a paycheck to balance their family commitments. And in health care, the 2006 reforms have smoothed the benefits cliff. Catamount Health provides a subsidy to purchase private insurance on a sliding scale basis.

We partnered with the Social Security Administration on a work incentive pilot program for people who receive Social Security Disability Insurance benefits. Beginning in 2004, the pilot began helping disabled Vermonters return to work without fear of being cut off from benefits for doing so. For every $2 beneficiaries earn above a certain wage threshold, only $1 is reduced from the benefits they receive. Six years in, the program has been a tremendous success. In 2010, when the federal government decided to expand the pilot, Vermont was chosen to continue its participation.

The demand is ever-growing and, without modernizing the delivery system and our programs, we will not be able to adequately keep pace. Particularly during a recession, even the best-managed programs need to be examined and revitalized. Under Global Commitment, we have demonstrated that we can, in fact, do better by spending less, if we focus our resources more thoughtfully.

The work of modernizing and improving programs is never done. Those who resist change ultimately put the long-term viability of our social safety net at risk. The capacity of taxpayers to foot the bill is not unlimited and we must balance the cost of our system with our ability to provide the best social program: a good job.

Struggling Taxpayers

Vermont is among the most heavily taxed states in the nation. While we are rightly proud of the high quality services we provide to those most in need, we must also remain cognizant of the burden of taxation and the impact it has on our economic competitiveness. During my tenure, I have looked for opportunities to reduce the burden on overly taxed Vermonters. That is why I have been so outspoken about the need to address our level of taxation.

The most enduring and intractable tax challenge we face is the property tax. Vermont has long struggled with how best to fund education. As taxpayers, we spend more on public education than any other government program. Furthermore, we have among the highest property taxes in the nation. In 1997, in response to the Vermont Supreme Court's landmark decision in Amanda Brigham v. State of Vermont, Act 60 was enacted, fundamentally changing K through 12 education funding. The Court's decision caused Vermont to move from a system where funds for education were primarily raised at the local school district level by a local property tax with state funds used to subsidized poorer school districts, to a statewide system funded primarily through statewide revenues, including a statewide property tax.

With over 250 separate school districts, the transformation was a jolting experience for many Vermonters. Within the machinery of Act 60 was a redistributive mechanism known as the "sharing pool." This fractured approach to education funding caused deep divisions in our state. To remedy some of the divisiveness inherent in Act 60, I proposed changes my first year in office. Act 68 was the ultimate outcome of those proposals. Most significantly, Act 68 eliminated the "sharing pool," which caused so much rancor in the Act 60 system.

But Act 68 only went so far. As I said after signing the legislation into law: "There is more work to do. The tax relief that Vermonters will receive will be short-lived unless we return to finish the work of addressing the rampant increases in the cost of education." Since the 2003 reforms, not enough progress has been made in controlling school spending. The benefits of Act 68 were, indeed, short lived.

The fundamental problem with Act 60 and Act 68 is that school district voters determine the level of spending, but the Legislature and the governor must raise the associated revenues. This structural disconnect between the decision to spend and the responsibility to pay has had the expected result of increasing school spending at a rapid rate, even though the population of K through 12 students has dropped dramatically. Further, our generous income sensitivity provisions shield most voters from the consequences of their spending decisions, while shifting the burden to others, particularly businesses, making it more difficult to create jobs in Vermont.

From 1997 through 2008, statewide school spending has grown from $834 million to nearly $1.5 billion, or 75 percent, at an annual growth rate of 5.2 percent. During this same period, school enrollment dropped by nearly 12 percent and school staffing grew by 25 percent, causing the rate of spending per pupil to grow at the fast pace of 6.9 percent per year. Vermont has the lowest ratio of pupils to teachers and pupils to staff among the 50 states.

In the face of rapid spending growth, which has driven property taxes to among the highest in the nation, and the demographic shift occurring in our schools, I offered proposals from 2006 to 2010 to bring spending to more sustainable levels. While some small victories were achieved, the Legislature has not acted on major structural changes to provide needed relief to property tax payers. At some point, the relentless march of higher spending in the face of fewer students will reach a tipping point, forcing us to confront a fiscal crisis.

Sacrifice Must Be Shared Broadly

When the global economic downturn hit Vermont in 2008, we didn't know whether it would be a quick dip or long slowdown. The truth was much worse than either scenario: a protracted recession worse than anything since the Great Depression. Within six months, we went from an economy streaming along to a freefall. State revenues dropped off precipitously and spending needed to be reined in quickly. From the early months of 2008 until I left office, all of our efforts were focused on getting our economy back on track while keeping budgets in balance.

Tax receipts into state coffers reveal how swiftly and how deeply the economy faltered. General Fund revenues topped off in fiscal year 2008 at $1.2 billion dollars. By fiscal year 2010, revenues had dropped almost 14 percent to just above $1 billion and were not expected to reach 2008 levels again until 2013. This revenue decline – combined with an increased demand for state programs that were already teetering on the brink – led to dramatic budget shortfalls. The budgets I submitted to the General Assembly for fiscal years 2010 and 2011 both closed gaps of over $150 million.

There were few acceptable solutions to manage a budget crisis of this magnitude. Like President George Bush, President Obama, and both Democratic and Republican leaders in Washington, I was convinced that raising taxes on already struggling workers and employers was the worst approach to closing the gap and helping the economy – especially in Vermont where residents already face one of the highest tax burdens in America. We also did not want to force a wholesale stop on social service programs that would hurt vulnerable Vermonters.

As a first step and a demonstration of leadership, my appointees and I took a 5 percent pay cut and would forgo pay increases for the remainder of my tenure. We cracked down on a range of expenses throughout state government.

Fortunately, the most difficult choices were bypassed because of an extraordinary federal response that supported states through increased funds for Medicaid and education and flexible funds for general government. The ARRA legislation was a critical lifeline to states dealing with double-digit percentage budget gaps. I cautioned the Legislature that ARRA funds should not take the place of tough budget decisions, but to use the federal money judiciously to avoid the worst case choices. Vermont needed to plan responsibly for the end of federal support; without that forethought, our budget would be on the edge of a steep cliff, forcing even more difficult decisions.

The budgets I presented contained a balance of structural reforms, innovative approaches, labor and retirement savings, and traditional reductions that protected critical services while responsibly bridging the gaps. Three key disagreements emerged with the Legislature: school spending, labor cost savings, and new taxes. By the end of the 2009 session, the Legislature decided to go its own way in its budget. I vetoed the spending measure and was overridden, resulting in more than $20 million in new taxes.

The fiscal challenges did not go away. With the Legislature's imposed budget we had a $154 million budget shortfall to contend with in the fiscal year 2011 budget. As was my responsibility, I offered a plan to address the shortfall and did so, again, without raising taxes. While it was the most difficult budget I crafted in my eight years in office, the task was made more manageable by efforts that began in the summer of 2009.

A panel convened to make recommendations on how to address growing pension liabilities came back with recommendations for $25 million in savings. Although the state employees union did not agree to any changes, the state's teachers' union agreed to a series of reforms resulting in $15 million in savings. But with such a large shortfall, every bit helped. For the first time since the State began collective bargaining in the 1970s, we negotiated a pay cut with state employees. The three percent reduction agreed to by the employees union contributed to $9 million in savings toward the budget shortfall, for which I was very grateful. In addition to the pension and pay reforms, the Legislature and my administration agreed to find $37 million through *Challenges for Change*.

After difficult negotiations through the 2010 session, I came to a budget agreement with legislative leaders and left the state with a balanced budget of which we can be proud. We maintained full reserves, protected the most vulnerable, made important reforms to state government and avoided tax increases. In fact, the final plan also rolled back two of the tax increases passed the year before – on capital gains and estates.

We also reformed our unemployment insurance program. Like many other states, the Great Recession has caused large shortfalls to develop in the fund. We needed to make adjustments to the wage-base that employers pay on, as well as to benefits, so the fund could return to solvency.

One area that went unaddressed in 2010 was education spending. The unwillingness to bend the curve on ever-growing school costs will continue to make it difficult to afford the many other necessities of state government.

The effects of the Great Recession will be felt for a long time and state government must continue to watch its expenditures closely. Revenues will not likely return to pre-recession levels until 2013 or later, but Vermont remains in a strong position with full reserves, a strong bond rating, a manageable shortfall and pension reforms already underway. The fiscal foundation of our state is solid.

◆ ◆ ◆

The state budget is the blueprint for our priorities. It is the foundational document of state government. Every expenditure, from education to environmental protection and from economic development to public safety, must be balanced among others within the collective ability of Vermonters to pay. As John F. Kennedy said, "To govern is to choose."

From the day I took office, my strategy has been to invest in Vermonters. What we pay for says much about us. Vermonters are caring; we have the most generous social safety net in the country. Vermonters are innovative; we are considered a national leader in health care reform. Vermonters are environmentally conscientious; we have made unprecedented investments to clean our lakes and streams. Vermonters take care of those who protect them; we continue to strongly support our public safety professionals.

We are not perfect in deciding how and where to spend money – no one is. There is always a better way. Throughout my years I looked to areas where we could do and should do better. That is why I proposed an unprecedented commitment to helping our next generation get the education they need to compete in a rapidly changing economy. We still must do more to make higher education more affordable. It is why I committed our state to the path of universal access to cell phone and broadband services. We have prioritized investments and attracted the necessary funding to achieve our goal. Now we must finish the job.

On a fundamental level, investing in Vermonters means not asking them for more than they can provide. The most effective way to invest in people is to let them invest in themselves, in our economy and our future. The ingenuity and hard work of those who call this place home is constrained only by the barriers government puts in their way. That is why I worked to contain the excesses of government and relieve Vermonters from their heavy tax burden.

To be sure, there is a necessary role for government. There is a level of taxation that is required to provide for the public good. But government must always be humble in what it deems worthy of doing. Public servants must always ask, "Are taxpayers getting the best value for their investment in government?"

Vermonters at War

"We strive to share the virtues of our forbearers, those values of hard work, honesty, courage and sacrifice. There is no finer group of Vermonters who exemplify and embody those qualities than the men and women who defend our freedoms and protect our homes and neighborhoods. They are guardians of liberty, keepers of security and their uncommon sacrifice must never go unappreciated."
— Third State of the State Address, 2008 —

WHEN I ASSUMED office in early 2003, American troops were already in Afghanistan, and we were on the verge of another war in Iraq. I knew that as Commander in Chief of the Vermont National Guard I had a responsibility to support the brave men and women who serve our state and nation. What I did not know at the time was that the Global War on Terror (GWOT) would extend the length of my tenure with countless deployments, homecomings, charity events, two trips to the war zones to visit our troops and, of course, the sorrowful funerals of those who did not make it home. Indeed, war was not something that I believed would be such a significant part of my governorship.

I knew as soon as the first of our National Guard was called up for duty that we had to act quickly to ensure that we had the necessary systems in place to support our soldiers and their families in this difficult time. Not only would our men and women face the realities of war overseas, but many were also leaving their spouses, children and jobs here at home.

Shortly after United States forces entered Iraq in the spring of 2003, I made it a priority to reorganize and strengthen my Governor's Veterans Advisory Council to ensure that our soldiers get the help and support they need. This Council has served me and all Vermonters well with its wealth of experience and advice on all the many complex and often hidden issues facing returning warriors.

Veterans of all wars and eras deserve to be treated as the heroes they are. They have put their lives on the line to assure our nation's security, and the freedom and liberty we so enjoy. But the growing engagement of the National Guard, in multiple and prolonged deployments in both Iraq and Afghanistan, has created other very real issues. To address these challenges, we have created programs and strengthened others to empower our service men and women and their families so that they can successfully reintegrate into their communities upon their return.

I wanted to assure that those returning to civilian life had a complete yet simple resource that would lay out all the many programs designed to assist them, whether federal, state or private. The result was the *Vermont Thank You Booklet* that became a national model emulated by states like Illinois, Pennsylvania and New York. This booklet serves as a reference guide for soldiers and their families.

Of course, we want to assure that those returning from the war have all their health needs taken care of, and that those with recognized or unrecognized post traumatic stress disorder receive treatment. On multiple occasions I convened those from the various state and federal agencies to assure that all were working together seamlessly, and that no veteran would fall through bureaucratic cracks.

For many years Vermont was the only state that did not assist veterans applying for disability benefits. In January 2005 Vermont created the first Veteran Service Officer position, with a second to follow in January 2007, to assist veterans applying for disability benefits from the U.S. Department of Veterans Affairs. These positions were much needed and have been a valuable resource for our veterans. To date, this office has represented over 1,200 Vermont veterans seeking disability benefits, successfully advocating for 95 percent of them, and earning over $10 million in benefits.

We ensured the continued funding for the Vermont Casualty Assistance Program, providing support to the families of soldiers killed or wounded during the GWOT. This program, which has paid out over $80,000, was critical during the first few years of the GWOT before the federal government expanded its services to these families. In 2010 we created the *Vermont Veterans' Fund*, which will be funded through a state income tax return check-off.

Importantly, I wanted to assure that veterans of all wars understood how much we cherished their service and sacrifice. When I took office, over 800 veterans were waiting to receive state medals recognizing their service, and there were no funds to purchase additional sets. All of my budgets fully funded the medal program, and we eliminated the backlog in my first year in office. Since 2004 I have been honored to host an annual ceremony at the State House for veterans to receive their medals and be honored in person. We eliminated the fee for veteran recognition license plates and more plates were added to recognize veterans of past wars. In addition, a plate was created to recognize Gold Star families.

While we do all we can for our wounded warriors, we must never forget those service members, and their families, who made the ultimate sacrifice in defense of liberty and freedom. I am proud that we enacted the Armed Services Scholarship Act, which extended education benefits to survivors of military members who died in service, extended benefits to surviving spouses, and allowed survivors to use the scholarship at private colleges in Vermont.

I was honored on so many occasions to wish our soldiers and airmen well as they deployed on their long and dangerous missions. I could see the look of determination and pride and of soft sorrow as they kissed their loved ones goodbye. I was grateful for the opportunity to again meet with many of these brave men and women at their duty stations in Iraq, Afghanistan and Kuwait, and see first-hand their dedication, professionalism, and most importantly, the difference they were making to secure the freedom they were fighting to preserve.

One can never get used to receiving the news that one of our state's bravest has laid down his life. Vermont has mourned the loss of too many brave soldiers – more than our share of loss. Each time I've picked up the phone to console a grieving parent or spouse, I am reminded of the deep strength of our state and her people. I will never forget these brave warriors; indeed their sacrifice and their service will live on in Vermonters' hearts forever.

On November 11, 2010, I was honored to help dedicate the Global War on Terror memorial in Randolph. This memorial was the product of the determined leadership of the Vermont Fallen Families, in coordination with my Veterans Advisory Council, the Vermont Veterans Memorial Cemetery Advisory Board and Adjutant General Michael Dubie. This important memorial assures that those heroes who gave their lives for this nation will always have a place to be honored.

The National Guard had earlier dedicated its own memorial for Guard members killed in the Global War on Terror. Our commitment to honoring Veterans of past wars led to the rededication of an improved and expanded Vietnam Veterans Memorial in Sharon in 2005, and in 2004 named the Bennington Bypass as the World War II Veterans Memorial Highway, and in 2003 Route 7 in Southern Vermont was dedicated as the Korean War Veterans Memorial Highway.

Several other veterans' programs have been enacted or enhanced. Korean and Vietnam War era veterans now have the same opportunity as their World War II predecessors without a high school diploma to receive one from a Vermont public school of their choice; Vermont towns may now voluntarily increase their property tax exemption for disabled veterans from $20,000 to $40,000; and legislation was enacted that allows veterans to apply for state positions that would normally only be available to current state employees.

As a tangible sign of my commitment to our veterans, the budget for the Vermont Office of Veterans Affairs has been increased more than threefold over my eight years in office. I wanted to assure that this small but important office has the resources necessary to meet the growing demands of all veterans, those from days long past to those fresh from their return home.

We have always strived to give our full support and commitment to Vermonters in the armed services. State government, as an employer, has been part of this effort. In 2005, I was given the *Pro Patria* award from the Employer Support of Guard and Reserve (ESGR) and, in 2006, we received the *Freedom Award* – the top honor – from ESGR.

On a personal level, I was surprised and humbled to be made an honorary Green Mountain Boy by Adjutant General Dubie at a ceremony in December 2010. There are few higher honors.

I am proud of the vast network of programs and services expanded, created and provided to the men and women who serve our state so bravely now and in the past. I believe that it is our responsibility to afford them and their families every opportunity to reintegrate after war and achieve their dreams. I hope that these men and women always know how grateful I am for their selfless service and what an honor it has been to be their Commander in Chief.

The Unfinished Work

To sustain liberty, we must be willing to each give our own measure to preserve, protect and defend it. We have crafted a system of self-governance that requires leaders who value actions more than words, who can be bold but humble, and speak plainly the truth; leaders who have passion and patience, resilience and restraint; and, above all else, leaders who are unwavering in their commitment to the people they serve.

The work of democracy – our role in the constant cultivation of an ever more perfect union – is never done. We have the great responsibility of devoting ourselves to service so that we may build a better future for the next generation. I have tried to do that.

As I reflect on eight years as governor, I am proud of what we have done to advance the cause of service, to make our state more prosperous, to protect the most vulnerable and to ensure that access to government is not a privilege but a right for all people.

Serving as governor of Vermont has been an honor unmatched in my life. My will to lead, the courage to do what is right, and the determination to fight for those who do not have a voice is renewed from the strength of Vermonters I meet every day.

We are one community, joined by our common love of this great state. In the years to come, as I pass over the high gaps of the Green Mountains and draw in the full breadth of Vermont – from its flowing waters up to its majestic crowns – I will be forever thankful for this land we call home. There is no greater place and there are no greater people than those who have been blessed to live among her hills.

Thank you, my fellow Vermonters, for the privilege of serving as your governor. Thank you very much, indeed.

APPENDIX A

Selected Photographs

On the campaign trail with Brian Dubie, announcing my Plan for
Prosperity in September of 2002 in front of the old Bombardier plant
in Barre. Thanks in part to the VEGI program, Northern Power
Systems now makes wind turbine blades at the facility.

Dorothy and I are entering a packed Plumley Armory at Norwich
University to celebrate our first Inaugural Ball on January 11, 2003. We
held four balls during my tenure, raising money for the United Way,
military family organizations and the Vermont Foodbank.

At a ceremony on the State House lawn honoring veterans from every
conflict since World War II with the Vermont Veterans Medal on
June 13, 2004.

The ritual of the weekly press conference with Vermont media. This event from November 10, 2004 was to announce my appointment of Paul Reiber as the new Chief Justice of the Vermont Supreme Court.

I was out meeting Vermonters nearly every day of my tenure. In this
photo from February 2006, I was visiting with workers
at Vermont Gas Systems.

County fairs are a wonderful place to meet folks from all walks of life – plus sample the great local products Vermont has to offer. In this photo from July 2006, Dorothy and I stopped for a photo with friends at the Lamoille County Field Days.

Foreign investment has been important for job creation in Vermont.
On my June 2007 trip to Asia, I met with Shanghai Mayor Han Zheng.

Nearly every day during the legislative session, I held an "open door" in the Ceremonial Office for anyone to stop by and chat. Here I'm discussing the day's events with my Chief of Staff, Tim Hayward.

When skies darkened over the American economy, we acted fast. On April 18, 2008, I announced my Economic Growth Initiative as a first step to fight back.

As federal lawmakers discussed how to administer the massive recovery effort, I weighed in with Vice President Joe Biden on June 24, 2009 on how states would best be helped by any federal assistance.

Photo courtesy of The White House.

As Chair of the National Governors Association, I led the organization as Congress debated a major health care overhaul. Here with Gov. Joe Manchin (D-WV) at the NGA Winter Meeting on Feb. 22, 2010 in Washington DC. *Photo courtesy of the NGA.*

Dorothy and I enjoy a laugh with my staff in the Ceremonial Office.

With Premier Jean Charest, receiving l'Ordre national du Quebec,
on March 11, 2010. Strengthening Vermont-Quebec relations was a
proud achievement of my administration.

Signing my final bill on June 4, 2010. I signed over 750 bills as governor, and vetoed a few others.

Raising the battle flag with Vermonters in Afghanistan in July 2010. It was a tremendous privilege to visit our brave men and women on the battlefield and thank them for their service.

APPENDIX B

Selected Major Speeches

First Inaugural Address
January 9, 2003

Mr. President, Mr. Speaker, Mr. Chief Justice, Members of the General Assembly, distinguished guests, fellow Vermonters:

Today we begin anew as we celebrate our past and look forward to the future.

Nearly 11 and a half years ago, a young physician received a phone call informing him of the untimely death of a governor who had come to personify Vermont. He finished the examination, put down his stethoscope, removed his lab coat and traveled to Montpelier to take the oath that would transform him from an untested part-time lieutenant, into captain of the ship of state.

Today, like his predecessor, that doctor-Governor has come to exemplify Vermont. He will be remembered as a competent, compassionate and forthright leader who always sought to do right by the people. On behalf of a grateful state, thank you, Howard Dean, for your two decades of service to Vermont.

No one could be standing here today without the support of a loving family. Thank you, Mom and Dad, my two sons, Matt and Andrew, and thank you especially to Dorothy for your steadfast support and for all of your sacrifices.

We have traveled a great distance since the first Vermont government met in March 1778. At that time, there were no laws, no taxes, no agencies or departments, just a people determined to live free and by their own values.

Our very right to exist was challenged not only by the British, but by Revolutionary America itself. Within a few short years, however, the people of Vermont had not only secured our right to exist, but we were being welcomed as the fourteenth star on the flag of a nation that would come to be known as the greatest beacon of liberty in human history.

In the 225 years since that first government met we have faced many challenges. War has visited the Green Mountains on two occasions. National recessions periodically depleted our resources, and, temporarily, our aspirations. Natural disasters, like the 1927 flood, devastated the state, but reinforced our commitment to each other.

We have responded to our greatest challenges, not by putting aside our differences, but by building on our common understandings. Seeking that common understanding was what Vermont's founders called civic virtue.

I am a graduate of this House. Thirty years ago this week I took my seat as a representative from Middlebury. America was in the midst of a long and divisive war and a presidency was crumbling under the weight of scandal inspired by politics run awry. But here, tucked among the rolling hills of Vermont, under this dome, men and women of goodwill met and progress triumphed over partisanship.

I pledge to you that I will carry on the Vermont tradition of civic virtue. I will be a willing listener and a reasonable partner. My intentions will be sincere, my word will be my bond, and while we may not always agree on approach, our goals are shared.

We are confronted today with challenges of great proportions.

The people have tasked us with bridging our differences to meet common ideals. Chief among those ideals is restoring the hope, opportunity, and dignity that come with a good and secure job.

An extended economic slowdown has indiscriminately cast thousands of Vermonters into unemployment, and a cloud of uncertainty lingers on the horizon as our economy teeters precariously between recession and recovery. For too many of our neighbors, high hopes have turned to deep concerns and the bright promise of a new century has been dimmed by anxiety about the future.

Making recovery more difficult is the reputation Vermont has earned as a particularly challenging place to do business and create jobs. This is a burden not borne for long by large employers. They can always find someplace else eager to accommodate them.

But the burden that large businesses can escape falls hard on small businesses, and especially on the working men and women of this state who have few options. They can uproot their families and follow the jobs – and many have – or they can wait for a change – and many do.

And so my message to the people of Vermont is change begins today – not change for the sake of change, but change for the sake of progress.

The change I have called for, and which the people have affirmed, will not come overnight. My vision for Vermont's economic future is not one of quick fixes or government gimmicks. It is one of careful consideration, common sense planning and prioritizing, and a new role for government that puts power back in the hands of people.

After all, government does not create jobs, people do. But government can encourage economic growth by fostering an environment that welcomes job creation, bolsters business, promotes commerce and serves people.

Conditions such as the ones we face today require that we take a close look at what we can do to improve not only the economy, but also the government. Tough times like these reveal where government's good intentions can fall short of sound and sustainable budgeting.

Fiscal responsibility means not only planning for today, but also planning for an uncertain tomorrow. And so we are rightly charged not only with addressing today's afflictions, but we are morally obligated to address impending deficits that will burden our children if we do nothing. We must begin to act now.

In two weeks I will propose a budget that will avert a deficit that would delay recovery and threaten future prosperity. It will also begin to slow the planned growth of government in future years which, left unrestrained, would endanger programs critical to the most vulnerable among us. The greatest threat to these important programs is not from those who would restrain them, but from those who would allow them to grow so big that they collapse under the burden of their own weight. I reserve the bulk of my remarks on the budget and other subjects until later this month, but let me be clear: the choices ahead will not be easy.

I would also remind you that state government is not alone in facing tough times. Thousands of Vermont's families have to balance their budgets despite less income, and they expect us to as well; we must not bend to the temptation of dipping even further into their pocketbooks to do it.

As we begin the task of putting Vermonters back to work, let us take stock of our assets. We have two great economic advantages – our natural environment and Vermonters themselves.

Generations of Vermonters have been blessed by a landscape that nourishes the soul. We are a leader among states and nations in protecting the quality of our water and air, and we will continue in that role.

There are some, sincere but misguided, who would have us believe that jobs exist at the expense of the environment. There are others, equally sincere and equally misguided, who believe that environmental protection comes at the expense of economic progress.

However, the choice we face today is not a choice between jobs or the environment. It is a choice between both or neither. I believe in a third way – The Vermont Way – that recognizes the codependence of our economy and our environment. My administration will work on behalf of each so that we may improve on both.

President Coolidge spoke of the Vermont appeal when at Bennington he made these memorable remarks: "I love Vermont because of her hills and valleys, her scenery and invigorating climate, but most of all, because of her indomitable people."

It is the people of Vermont who represent our greatest hope and best opportunity for a brighter tomorrow. It is the construction worker, the nurse, the firefighter and the farmer, the teacher and the student on whose foundation we prepare to build a future of prosperity. Our people are blessed with creative minds, industrious hands, common sense and a determined spirit.

I will seek their guidance, rely on their wisdom and trust in their judgment. I will listen to them, and in order to get our state back on track, I will invest in them – in their education, in their skills and in their entrepreneurial spirit.

The moment is fitting to remind ourselves that as officers of government we are servants of the people, one and all; that our authority is derived from them, and therefore, as our Constitution demands, we are "at all times...accountable to them."

I shall instruct all who serve in my administration of the same as we endeavor toward government that works with you, not against you; a government that serves as an ally, not an adversary. I will seek to change the culture of government from one that is so attached to the status quo it resists even those changes that will move us forward, to one that embraces positive change.

We are in the infancy of an era of technological progress that has changed the way the world does business. Government, too, must change the way it does business. We must better utilize technology to improve the convenience and accessibility of government services. Across the government, we can do more so Vermonters can save time by being online rather than in line.

Vermont's economy has been slow to make the transition to the 21st Century. We have not fully embraced advances that make it possible for Vermonters to operate in a diverse, high-wage economy, even while working from the most remote corner of the Northeast Kingdom.

Cutting-edge clean technologies have sprouted businesses that do not compete with the environment, but rather compete with each other to achieve a cleaner environment. Welcoming these businesses to Vermont, and encouraging their innovation and growth will allow us to promote Vermont values around the nation, and indeed around the world.

We must embrace innovation all around us. Creative ideas can expand access to affordable health care to every Vermonter; improve quality, comfort, and convenience, while giving patients and doctors more control over health care decisions.

New approaches can improve our schools while increasing the role of parents in their children's education. Working families need to know that their young children will have the early care and education they need to thrive. And they need to know that their kids are getting a truly equal opportunity at success.

Act 60 promised equal educational opportunity for every child while reducing property taxes. Instead, many of our children are still not receiving the education their parents are paying for, even as property taxes continue to skyrocket.

We need to work together to find a better solution – a solution that recognizes the importance of money, but also recognizes that our commitment to equal educational opportunity is not fulfilled by funding formulas, sharing pools and block grants.

If we are serious about every child attending a safe and drug-free school; every child having access to the best teachers and the best curriculum; if we are serious about accountability; if we are serious about every child having an equal chance, shouldn't every parent have an equal choice?

My administration will seek to unleash the pent up creative energies of a people frustrated by unnecessary barriers to opportunity. We will start by fixing a broken permitting system that has become too costly, duplicative, unpredictable and often times contradictory, not by weakening our commitment to the environment, but by strengthening our commitment to common sense.

When we speak of economic progress let us not forget the industry upon which Vermont was built and which, in a changing economy, we have too long neglected. Let us renew our commitment to the family farmers who have contributed so much to Vermont's character and whose lives are dedicated to feeding others, but who now struggle to sustain themselves.

I have spoken about ways to expand opportunity for Vermonters. But today hope and opportunity are being destroyed by the insidious effects of hard-core drugs. By now, we've all heard of families and lives torn apart by drugs. I am reminded of "Sarah," a 19-year-old Vermonter who died of a heroin overdose. Sarah was a typical kid with big plans for the future. She was working two jobs with plans to go to college and eventually open a business of her own.

But alcohol, then marijuana and cocaine clouded her horizons. Before long, heroin found Sarah, and the sun set on what was once a promising life.

For a moment, I want you to think not just of Sarah, but of your own children and what could happen if they meet the wrong person on a particularly tough day. Sarah's story isn't the story of just one girl, but of a growing number of Vermont's young people.

We must do more to protect our children from the life-destroying effects of these drugs. Some of it is tough love, and some of it is just plain love. We will address addiction with a compassionate program of treatment and rehabilitation. And we will educate kids about the dangers of drug abuse so they will have the strength and courage to reject them.

But we will also aggressively combat those who would seek to poison our children for profit. All drug dealers will know that they are unwelcome on our streets, in our neighborhoods, around our schools – anywhere in our state.

With change comes great opportunity. But we must also fiercely defend the values that are woven deep into the fabric of our state.

The best of Vermont is the product of those unchanging ideals of family, faith, freedom and unity. There is little government can do that can match the compassion of the family; nothing it can do to match the power of faith.

For freedom, generations of Vermonters have fought heroically at home and abroad – at home to gain independence and end slavery. Abroad to defeat totalitarianism and fascism; and today, across the globe, to vanquish evil and terror. To the men and women who loyally guard our freedom, we thank you for your courage and sacrifice.

While Ethan Allen and the Green Mountain Boys made famous Vermonters' attachment to individual freedom and liberty, we are united in our common concern for the most vulnerable among us. Our rural nature has always instilled in Vermonters an independent spirit, but it has also encouraged a sense of obligation to neighbors in need. We are proud to do for ourselves all that we can, and eager to aid others where they cannot.

Around our state, dedicated Vermonters work together to heal the sick, feed the hungry, and protect the weak. These times call for a renewed sense of service to the community and there is plenty for everyone to do. I ask all Vermonters to dedicate more of their time and talent to worthy causes.

Nor shall we in this chamber forget our obligations to do for others those necessary things they cannot do for themselves. Let our own examples here restore faith in government as a noble calling, and inspire other honest, wise and good citizens to public service. The challenges ahead are difficult. In some areas, progress will be slow, but it is certain.

And so today we celebrate a new beginning and begin to implement the change for which the people have called. We will keep what has worked, discard what has failed, rein in our excesses and proceed forward with a bold agenda of renewal.

When I arose today, it was cold and dark. The sun had not yet reached the eastern shores of New England nor begun its climb over the Green Mountains.

As I have for the past 30 years, I traveled through the morning darkness on the journey from my home in Middlebury over Appalachian Gap to Montpelier. As I began to wind along the mountain road the darkness slowly waned and pine boughs emerged from under a shroud of snow. Not even the frost of winter could dim the color of our hills or restrain the advancing dawn.

So long as we serve, so long as we strive, so long as we have the courage to lead, the promise of Vermont will remain ever green. Our promise will be strengthened by the seasons – through the bitter winters and the brilliant mornings – and made eternal in the sacrifice we share.

Together, and with God's help, we shall meet the challenges ahead, as we have all others, so we may welcome a springtime of hope and a blossoming of opportunity to this "brave little state of Vermont."

Thank you.

2004 State of the State
January 6, 2004

MR. PRESIDENT, MR. Speaker, distinguished Members of the General Assembly, my fellow Vermonters:

The year 2004 is upon us and it is my honor to report to you on the condition of our state, the progress we have made in the past year and the ambitious agenda that lies ahead.

When I first addressed you from this podium a year ago, Vermont was in the midst of difficult times and a quiet anxiety persisted among the working people of our state. Job losses and plant closings were daily reminders that something was not right, and it was the judgment of the people that it was time for a change – a change in approach, a change in focus and a change in tone.

They demanded we take a critical look at the policies of the past and work together to craft new solutions for the future. So I asked you to join me in achieving change in a new spirit of civic virtue that valued cooperation over contention, and it is with great satisfaction that I stand with you today and say that progress has indeed triumphed over partisanship.

As a result of our measured dialogue, professionalism, bipartisanship, and genuine goodwill, the people of Vermont will recall of this past year that this administration and this General Assembly were partners for positive change. It is my expectation that we who join here to answer the call to public service will continue in this spirit.

Today, the change the people called for is underway, and it is helping to lift the cloud of uncertainty that lingered too long on our horizon.

Vermont's economy is strengthening. At only 4 percent, our unemployment rate is the fifth lowest in the nation and nearly 2 points lower than the national average.

While other states experienced severe deficits that caused them to raise taxes and slash vital services, we produced a balanced budget, and Vermont is among only a handful of states to end the most recent fiscal year in surplus. We did it all while protecting the most vulnerable among us and without raising the net tax burden on the people.

We were able to maintain fiscal responsibility by holding the growth in general fund spending to the lowest level in a decade. By resisting the expansion and creation of expensive government programs, we ensured a more stable and sustainable fiscal future for our children. Let us continue to have the courage to stand firm.

In one short year, we helped spur job creation by delivering the largest single economic stimulus bill in Vermont's history, providing over $105 million in new capital and tax incentives for employers, and training programs for workers.

We saved jobs in all four corners of the state and encouraged employers to invest in the creation of over 2000 good paying jobs for the years ahead.

We took steps to improve the arteries of a healthy economy – our roads and bridges – that over the last decade were allowed to deteriorate; and we stood up to the special interests and kept our promise to kick-start critical infrastructure projects like the Circ Highway that have been delayed by litigation, red tape and lack of will.

I offered an alternative to the often heated contest between those who seek economic growth and those who seek environmental preservation. This third way resists the extreme impulses of ideology and recognizes that in Vermont, our economy and environment are codependent. We must accommodate each for the betterment of both.

I laid out an ambitious plan for the clean up of Lake Champlain and waterways throughout the state. We spoke out strongly against plans to weaken regulations on coal-burning Mid-West power plants that contribute to air pollution in Vermont. We passed a long-awaited renewable energy bill to promote the use of renewable alternatives and offer consumers more renewable options; and we continue the fight to prevent a toxic tire-burn across the lake.

We turned years of rhetoric about combating Vermont's substance abuse problem into reality by passing my D.E.T.E.R. anti-drug program. We put more emphasis on prevention, more support behind community coalitions, more of the addicted in treatment, more counselors in our schools, more police on the streets, and more drug dealers behind bars – and we will not shrink from our responsibility to do more still.

We ended years of gridlock, and took the first steps to address the stifling burden of property taxation on our working families by passing Act 68. This dramatic reform eliminated the divisive sharing pool and will bring property tax relief to the vast majority of property owners.

We renewed our commitment to the family farm, providing farmers with emergency relief and eliminating the property tax on farm buildings in the Current Use program.

We took innovative steps to reduce the cost of prescription drugs by initiating the first-in-the-nation multi-state bargaining pool, and are aggressively pursuing strategies to gain access to less expensive Canadian pharmaceuticals.

We fortified the hospital regulatory process to prevent future abuses, and took aggressive steps to strengthen the credibility and accountability of Vermont's only academic medical center.

My administration has undertaken a massive reorganization of the Agency of Human Services to improve the way it serves Vermonters, and established the Vermont Institute for Government Effectiveness, a top to bottom review of government operations to root out waste and inefficiencies that cost taxpayer dollars.

And we are taking important steps to address the chronic and shameful neglect of important institutions like our State Hospital and our correctional facilities to ensure the safety and proper treatment of those in the care of the state.

This is a record of accomplishment of which we can all be proud.

As 2004 begins we have delivered on the promise of change for the sake of progress, in every agency of government, in every corner of the state, and for the benefit of every Vermonter. I am proud to report that the State of Vermont is strong and growing stronger.

We must pause today and acknowledge those Vermonters who every day risk their lives to protect us. We live in a time of extraordinary courage and sacrifice. I have had the privilege of thanking and helping to send off nearly every Vermont National Guard member and Reservist who has been deployed to defend us from terrorists and tyrants who seek to deliver their hate to our shores.

Six Vermonters have given their last full measure of devotion in the war to liberate Iraq. We will be eternally grateful for their sacrifice.

Here at home we rely on the women and men of the fire and rescue services and our federal, state and local law enforcement agencies who are committed to protecting us and responding to any crisis in our communities. Sadly, we lost two law enforcement officers, a first responder and a firefighter in the line of duty this past year.

Let us remember those we have lost, and join in honoring and thanking the members of our armed services and public safety community.

Our state is growing stronger and our economy is improving. But for those Vermonters who still struggle to find work the recession continues and to them I pledge my continued resolve. I will not be satisfied until every Vermonter who wants a job has a job.

A good job is more than just a paycheck. A good job fosters independence and discipline, and contributes to the health of the community. A good job is a means to provide for the health and welfare of your family, to own a home, and save for retirement. And a job is a source of dignity, hope and possibility for the future.

As I meet with Vermonters on factory floors throughout the state, I can see the difference that we have already made in people's lives.

Several weeks ago I had the pleasure of visiting Vermont Tubbs in Brandon to meet their dedicated employees and share with them my job creation agenda. The company was one of many that in the recent past was teetering on the brink of closure – an event that would cost our state roughly 200 jobs, including that of Serge Cotnoir.

Serge is a dedicated, hardworking Vermonter who cares about his family, his craft, his community and his state. In 2002, Serge lost his job in Island Pond when his plant closed. He was lucky enough to find a new job at Vermont Tubbs. Before long, however, continued economic stagnation put that job in jeopardy as well and it seemed to be a foregone conclusion that Vermont Tubbs would close its doors forever.

But through the determined efforts of the community, assisted by my administration, most of the jobs at Vermont Tubbs were saved and the employees of the company continue to produce some of the highest quality furniture in the world. Serge, who remains gainfully employed because of our efforts, epitomizes the honest, hard-working Vermonter whom we should keep uppermost in our minds as we conduct our work here during this coming session. Please join me in welcoming Serge, who is with us in the balcony today.

All Vermont workers can gain comfort from knowing that as long as I am governor, not a single job will be forfeited due to a lack of interest from Montpelier. We will fight for each and every one.

We will continue to invest in the skills and entrepreneurial spirit of Vermonters. They are the job creators, the workers, the thinkers, and the risk-takers.

As a next step toward improving our economy, I am proposing a series of initiatives that build on my plan for prosperity.

Last year, we took steps to reduce property taxes, and this year my administration is recommending that we lower property tax rates an additional 5 cents.

I asked the Tax Department to undertake a review of our entire tax structure to identify ways to reform the system to make it fairer for the everyday Vermonter. What we found will come as no surprise to most taxpayers – income tax rates in Vermont are simply too high. And it probably also comes as no surprise to find that our system is designed in a way that allows some to avoid paying their fair share. A system such as the one we have today discourages economic growth, creates cynicism and breeds resentment among our people.

So today, I am proposing reforms to Vermont's tax policy that will make our system of taxation more fair and equitable for all. My plan reduces personal income taxes across the board, while most significantly reducing the tax burden on low and middle income Vermonters – they are the people who need it most.

Vermont's middle income tax rate is currently 8th highest in the nation. Under my proposal, middle income Vermonters would see a 6.9 percent reduction in their income tax rate, dropping it to the more competitive rank of 16th in the nation.

The lower income tax rates I am proposing can be accommodated though common sense changes that will make our tax system fairer. Two years ago, Vermont adopted a measure exempting 40 percent of capital gains income, giving capital gains preferential treatment, and primarily benefiting the wealthiest taxpayers. Vermont is one of only five states that offer a broad-based exclusion for capital gains. In order to reduce income tax rates on all taxpayers, especially low and middle-income Vermonters, I am proposing to eliminate the 40% capital gains exemption except when the capital gain is associated with the transfer of farm property that will remain in production.

I also propose reducing the corporate income tax rate on employers to make them more competitive and to help them grow our economy and create good jobs. Vermont's top corporate income tax bracket is currently 5th highest in the nation. Our high rates handicap the state's ability to recruit employers and represent a significant competitive disadvantage for homegrown Vermont companies.

To make Vermont more competitive, strengthen our recruitment efforts and level the playing field, I am proposing that we reduce our corporate tax rates across the board an average of 14 percent.

This reduction will be phased in starting in 2006. With this change, Vermont's top corporate income tax rate will drop from 5th highest to 16th in the nation. These lower rates will be accomplished by closing loopholes in our tax code that allow some multi-state corporations to redirect profits to other states to avoid declaring them in Vermont. As a result, these huge companies pay only a minimum $250 tax while our homegrown Vermont businesses – particularly our small businesses – pick up the rest of the tab. These few multi-state corporations utilizing income-shifting strategies to avoid paying their fair share will see their taxes rise, while the typical Vermont employer will see its taxes drop significantly.

Taken together with my proposal to reduce the income tax burden on low and middle-income families, this tax reform program makes our system more fair and represents a better deal for all Vermonters.

I am also proposing additional marketing assistance and educational opportunities for small business owners, and we will resume our work to reform the permitting process and workers' compensation system.

In addition, we must cultivate the next generation of manufacturing to help replace the thousands of old-line manufacturing jobs that have disappeared over the past several years.

Therefore, we must support the development of high-tech centers through-out Vermont and the University of Vermont's efforts to develop an incubator facility for emerging technologies.

To help ensure the success of rural and urban employers alike, we must also build a robust technological infrastructure. Working with private sector partners we will create a wireless network that covers all of our major transportation arteries, and extend broadband Internet access to 90 percent of our homes and businesses by 2007.

And of course, we must continue to build on our relationship with our neighbors to the north. I want to thank Lt. Governor Brian Dubie for reopen-ing our door to Quebec and all of Canada. The opportunities for enhanced trade are great, benefiting us all.

We cannot discuss Vermont's jobs environment without discussing our nat-ural environment. Vermont's environment is where we work and play; where we hunt, fish, and trap; where we ski and ride; where we raise our children and make our way of life.

It is in this harmony, of the practicable and the pristine, that I have offered a third way – the Vermont Way – to balance the environmental protection we cherish with the needs of working Vermonters.

Over the past year, I have advanced an aggressive environmental agenda that embraces the Vermont Way. In September, I introduced my Clean and Clear Water Action Plan, a 6-year, $150 million commitment to accelerate the clean up of Vermont's waterways.

I have proposed starting the clean up in Lake Champlain, which has been plagued by a dangerous algae bloom that, during the summer months, has turned some areas into a thick, green muck.

My plan takes the first tangible measures in recent memory to mitigate per-sistent pollution problems in our lakes, rivers, and streams, and I look forward to the Legislature's support in this ambitious effort. We all share the goal of clean water, and want to achieve this goal as fast as possible.

The debate over stormwater runoff is complicated, but it is one we must resolve, and resolve quickly, with bipartisan support. While we struggle to find a solution, a Vermonter struggles to find a job, a family struggles to buy a home, and stormwater continues to pollute unabated. This General Assembly should not adjourn until the stormwater impasse is broken and we have found a solution.

In Vermont, it is natural that our discussions of development are steeped in the principles of responsible growth. This fall, I announced a collaborative effort to explore ways to formalize smart growth planning and speed the creation of designated opportunity centers. It is my goal that these opportunity centers offer permitting and tax incentives for businesses wishing to grow in Vermont. The Winooski downtown redevelopment is a good example of the smart growth model, and my administration will continue to support that important project.

The high cost of energy continues to be a critical issue for Vermonters. Last year, at my urging, the Legislature passed the Renewable Energy Bill that establishes "Renewable Energy Goals" and gives direct incentives to Vermonters who install renewable energy systems in their homes or businesses. I remain committed to the ongoing public dialogue and exploring all energy options as we discuss the future of power in Vermont.

One way to reduce electric bills, and contribute to environmental protection, is to conserve energy. State government must be an innovator in conservation and efficiency. We cannot expect families and businesses to conserve power if government fails to lead.

In the coming weeks, I will set forth a far-reaching plan to transform state government into a role model for environmental stewardship. We will reduce the impact of state government's daily activities and, in turn, increase market demand for environmentally sensitive products and services. This plan will include a new management system for the state's fleet of vehicles. With this ambitious strategy, we will aim to reduce government's contribution of greenhouse gasses by 25%, more than 34,000 tons of pollutants, by 2012.

Our deep respect for the land and its harvest is the legacy of generations of farmers who put food on our tables, preserved our landscape, and inspired us with a powerful work ethic.

Farming is a difficult way to make a living. Workdays often extend from darkness to darkness. In recent years, especially for our dairy farmers, even the longest day has not been enough to keep many farms profitable.

Beginning last year on my recommendation, the state took a more active role to help farms withstand hard times. We must remain unyielding in our support for the family farmers who contribute so much to our way of life.

Opportunities abound to encourage the diversification of agriculture in Vermont by supporting organic production, agri-tourism and the burgeoning specialty food industry that add value to farming operations. By helping our farmers pursue these strategies, working to strengthen Vermont's right to farm law, and continuing to offer them the assistance they need to weather difficult times, we can help ensure a bright future for the farm community and our entire state.

To ensure the brightest possible future for every Vermonter, however, we must address the growing problems of our health care system. We are fortunate to have a medical community and hospitals that provide high quality care. But ask any Vermonter and he or she will tell you that our health care system is ailing. Costs are too high, mandates too many and options too few.

Policymakers have struggled with this important issue for decades. In addressing this challenge, there are no easy answers, no silver bullets, no cure-all tonics; only tough choices. True reform must be comprehensive and address the totality of this problem.

Recent attempts by government to make health care more affordable and accessible have had unintended consequences that aggravated many of the ills it sought to cure.

Initial efforts started us down a hopeful path, but the true costs of that course are now becoming evident – insurance companies have fled our state leaving our residents with fewer choices, premiums have skyrocketed, doctors and hospitals are not receiving the reimbursements they were promised, patients are losing direct control over their care, and state-run programs are headed for collapse.

As government looks to solve a problem that government itself helped create, we must not allow the remedy to be more harmful than the disease. Any reasonable measure to improve the condition of Vermont's system and make healthcare more affordable must first "do no harm."

It must not raise the cost of care for the vast majority of Vermonters already insured through private insurance, nor should it raise taxes on already over-taxed workers. It must have long-term financial sustainability, improve access and open up competition among insurers to use market forces to drive costs down. And, finally, it should enhance the quality of care and put more power in the hands of doctors and patients, instead of government and health care bureaucrats.

This year, my administration has taken the initial steps toward real reform of Vermont's health care system. Right now, 78 percent of Vermont's health care dollars are going to treat patients with chronic illnesses such as diabetes, high blood pressure and cardiovascular disease. In partnership with Vermont's health care community, my administration launched a sweeping chronic care initiative designed to enhance treatment and lower costs for those with chronic illnesses and put the patient at the center of care.

We also began to look at long-term care for elderly and disabled Vermonters. $125 million of our state's healthcare budget supports these long term needs. By refocusing our delivery to home-based care we give seniors the choice they desire, increase the quality of care and reduce costs.

Just as we look to the oldest Vermonters, we must look to the youngest. The problem of childhood obesity is plaguing our youth. There is a direct relationship between obesity and a host of life-threatening maladies. My Fit and Healthy Kids Initiative is aimed at teaching the value of good nutrition and regular exercise to our youth through state leadership, community grants, and the establishment of the Green Mountain Games for Kids.

For all Vermonters, access to high-quality, low-cost prescription drugs is a priority. As part of my strategy for reducing the cost of pharmaceuticals, Vermont and Michigan formed the nation's first multi-state buying pool for prescription drugs in our Medicaid program, boosting the state's ability to get the best price for needed drugs. Further, we've been a national leader in petitioning the federal government for access to cheaper Canadian prescription drugs.

In a comprehensive approach, these are the first steps toward real reform. But, the most complex issue facing Vermont and the nation is the high cost of health insurance and the vicious cycle that pushes costs still higher as government seizes more control over the system. In the weeks ahead, I will present a series of carefully crafted proposals that will make improvements to the health care delivery system and make Vermont's health care laws more flexible so that consumers can have more low cost options that address their individual circumstances. These reforms will help increase access to affordable health care for all Vermonters, empower individuals with more direct control over their care, and work to save Medicaid for the most vulnerable.

The health and lives of too many Vermonters, especially our youth, are threatened by drug abuse.

For the first time, we have taken bold action to address Vermont's substance abuse problem. I am pleased to report that we are making extraordinary progress in treating it with a compassionate program that places a premium on prevention and targets our substance abuse resources where they are needed most.

As we gather here today, however, there are still schools that need counselors, communities that need recovery centers, prevention coalitions that need assistance, and addicts who need a treatment facility here in Vermont.

While we work to eliminate the demand for deadly drugs, we must also continue to pursue, arrest, prosecute, and punish those who push them.

For our state to succeed economically and culturally we must rely on the informed wisdom of our people, and we are duty bound to do all we can to help foster that wisdom through our system of public education.

Education is the great equalizer, giving the poor, the disadvantaged, the voiceless and the vulnerable the power to pursue their greatest hopes and aspirations so that no one may deny them their destiny.

Vermonters have demonstrated their devotion to this principle time and time again, seeking to balance funding among school districts, reduce class size and improve teacher pay, hoping to slowly but surely develop a system where all schools are capable of addressing all of our children's individual needs.

Vermont is fortunate to have so many wonderful and dedicated teachers and administrators who share this goal. Because of them our public school system is strong and it is a system of which we should be proud.

Despite all of our efforts, however, true equality of educational opportunity continues to escape too many of our children. It is our responsibility to ensure that these children have options so that not one day of learning is unnecessarily lost because of barriers erected by government.

Today, the children of wealthy Vermonters can escape such barriers by pay-ing tuition to another school of their choice. But for many middle and lower-income residents, tuition payments are not an option. Instead, they are forced to play the hand that is dealt them, and their child's future is on the line.

The time has come to find an alternative that gives every child, regardless of residence or economic background, a truly equal opportunity for a first class public education that meets his or her needs. School choice should not be a privilege reserved only for the wealthy. It should be the right of all Vermonters.

That is why I am proposing a statewide, K-12 public school choice program that affords all Vermont students an opportunity to attend the school of their choice. No longer can we allow the defenders of the status quo to stand in the way of equal access to the best education our public schools have to offer.

As you consider my proposal, you will hear testimony from parents whose children would benefit from choice. Their reasons will be diverse, but each equally important to their child. I urge you to listen to these families and the challenges they confront as they struggle to give their children access to the first-class education they deserve, and then pass a bill to guarantee it.

Over the last year, I've had the privilege of traveling the mountain gaps and green valleys of this great state.

Along the miles, I've met Vermonters on factory floors, in school cafeterias, and at backyard barbeques. I've met them on country roads, at county fairs, and church suppers.

I've met them in joy and in loss, in shining moments and in dark hours. I've met a strong people, full of dignity and resolve, from whom I draw inspiration, promise, and hope. It is for these everyday Vermonters, and for their struggle, that we push and pull to make this state a better place.

In my travels, I am reminded that the wellspring of Vermont liberty flows from Main Street, not State Street; from town meeting democracy, not govern-ment bureaucracy; and from the home of every Vermonter into this people's dome.

The agenda I offer is based on my many conversations with the people across this state. From their hopes and aspirations emerge the ideas that trans-form our society, sometimes brick by brick, and sometimes leap by bound. They are the true architects of my agenda. We have much to do – many more miles to go – and I welcome your partnership in this profound endeavor.

Thank you and may God bless you, our great state of Vermont, and the United States of America.

Second Inaugural Address
January 6, 2005

MR. PRESIDENT, MADAME Speaker, Mr. Chief Justice, Members of the General Assembly, distinguished guests, fellow Vermonters:

I am deeply honored to stand before you again and am humbled by the trust placed in me. I am proud to share this day with my family and especially my loving wife, Dorothy, and I thank them for their support throughout the years. I also want to thank Lt. Governor Dubie for his friendship, his leadership and his service to Vermont.

No person ever stands here alone. Even as I rose in this chamber for the first time, thirty-two years ago, as a freshman legislator, and raised my hand to take the oath of office, I stood tall on the shoulders of our ancestors.

Our forbears are the men and women of Vermont who battled to cut a living from her hills. From the tilled field and the ax swing came Vermonters' reputation for rugged individualism, hard work and personal industry; from harvesting the autumn bounty, the easy generosity of having just enough and no more than you need; from the Sunday trips to town, the power of faith and the spirit of community.

Our forbears worked hard this difficult land, and their reward was the freedom and independence of self-sufficiency. With this ethos, they charged their government to fill only the thin gaps left unfilled by community and family, recognizing, as they set forth in the Vermont Constitution, that "frequent recurrence to fundamental principles, and a firm adherence to justice, moderation, temperance, industry and frugality, are absolutely necessary to preserve the blessings of liberty, and keep government free."

I am lifted by the many things we've done to make Vermont better and stronger, protecting the most vulnerable while enabling individual growth and preserving essential liberty. In the last two years, we've worked together to bring hope where there was fear and opportunity where there was loss.

As I am encouraged with our progress, I know the many real challenges that face us and the steps we must take to meet them. Programs that were once intended to fill the thin gaps have expanded far beyond our means. We must take action to curb the unbridled growth of these programs and return them to their most vital purposes.

This is a task that will affect the Vermont we want a generation from now. It will set a course for the Vermont we will leave our children and grandchildren.

I see a Vermont where every individual is joined with opportunity; where every person who wants a job has a job; where dependence on government is not a way of life, but a temporary stop on the road to self-sufficiency.

I see a Vermont where every family is joined by compassion; where parents and children are united by understanding and unconditional love.

I see a Vermont where every community is joined by possibility; where caring hearts reach out to troubled souls; where every child enters school ready to learn and leaves school prepared to prosper; where the dream of homeownership is within reach of every family; where the grandeur of green mountains is the backdrop for downtowns bustling with commerce.

And I see a Vermont where our government is joined in a common purpose, bound by the shared values that make our state so special.

Today, I ask you to join me in a common purpose.

In my first inaugural message, I promised to initiate positive changes that would begin to address the challenges that faced Vermont, and I asked for the cooperation of a divided legislature. Together, we put progress over partisanship and accomplished much for the people of our state. I come before you again in the spirit of bipartisanship, asking you to join with me to advance our common goals and address our common challenges.

Our future success will be built on the solid foundation we've laid over the past two years. We made job creation a priority and our focus is paying off: more Vermonters are working and we have the lowest unemployment rate in the nation. For the first time in many years, employers see that Vermont is "open for business" and ready to be a partner in creating jobs.

We rejected the idea that job growth comes at the expense of our environment. Our permit reform measure brought the first meaningful changes to our regulatory system in thirty years and did so while affirming the environmental ethic Vermonters cherish. Our third way – the Vermont Way – is working and our economy is growing again.

We've made state government a leader in energy conservation. Through better fleet management and efficiency measures in state buildings, we'll stop hundreds of tons of pollutants from entering the atmosphere and save taxpayers millions. Our energy future is one of greater conservation and efficiency, and we will continue the robust dialogue on the diversity of alternative energy sources that best fit our state.

In the last biennium, we made a historic commitment to accelerate the clean up of Vermont's lakes and waterways. Key partners in our Clean and Clear initiative are the stewards of Vermont's landscape – our farmers. Every sip of milk, drop of syrup, and ear of corn is a testament to their hard work and tenacity, to which we all owe gratitude and thanks.

The General Assembly joined me in an unprecedented effort to give farmers emergency relief in a dark hour. The result is over one hundred family farms saved and many more lifted to financial security.

Other unsung environmental stewards are Vermont's hunters, anglers, and trappers who protect the values and traditions of outdoor sports in our state. Last year, we started to treat the plague of lamprey that are marring our fish. In the coming year, we must address the thinning deer herd to maintain the vitality of hunting in Vermont.

In the last biennium, we reformed Act 60 and we will continue to bring property tax relief to working Vermonters. We reaffirmed our commitment to time-honored uses of the land and the industries that thrive on it.

Two years ago, I challenged Vermont to confront the growing problem of illegal drug use among our youth. From all corners, the response was overwhelming and effects of our good work are being felt.

Through my DETER anti-drug program, the General Assembly is directing more resources for education, treatment, enforcement and rehabilitation. With the help of additional troopers, the State Police, working with sheriffs and local departments, are aggressively targeting out-of-state drug dealers and sending a message to the street that dealers are unwelcome in Vermont.

Our new high school drug counselors are reaching the at-risk population before it's too late and our specialists are helping addicts stay clean and rebuild their lives through expanded recovery programs around the state.

Several months ago, I had the opportunity to meet with three women at our new in-patient center in Bradford. They described their hard journey fighting addiction – the broken promises and bitter loneliness. But they spoke of the treatment center as someplace different, someplace where they could finally break free from the cycle of dependence. As I left, one of the women said to me, "For the first time in my life, I feel like someone cares about me."

But for all our progress, stories of grief remain. In recent months it has not been splashed across the headlines – but the addicted still face the quiet struggle – and their families still endure the quiet heartbreak. We must continue our fierce commitment to getting illegal drugs off our streets, away from our homes and out of our lives.

I was proud to sign a true Megan's Law for Vermont, a measure that established an online public registry of sex offenders so these violent criminals may no longer lurk anonymously in our neighborhoods.

But there is more we must do to help protect women and children against sexual predators. Vermont needs to enact a "civil commitment" law that ensures untreatable sex offenders are not released into the community to victimize again.

With all the challenges before us, let us pause to reflect on tragedy of an unthinkable magnitude half way around the world. Our thoughts and prayers go out to the victims and the families of the tsunami in South Asia.

Last week, I had the solemn honor of joining more than a thousand firefighters at the funeral of their colleague, Ray Davison, a great man and a great innovator in the fire service. His passing reminds us of the men and women who are first on the scene to our everyday disasters – all of the firefighters, police officers, and emergency service workers – and the constant thanks we owe them.

Right now, many of those first responders are answering a different call. They join their fellow Vermonters courageously serving our country and making our state proud in military operations around the world. We give our great respect and deep gratitude to all of these soldiers and their families for their sacrifice and service to our nation; and we remember those fallen and honor them for their courage and selflessness.

As these brave men and women fulfill their duty at home and abroad, it is our duty here to work together in common purpose to make the Vermont of their return even better than the Vermont they left behind.

As public servants, our chief responsibility is to build a government that is responsive to the needs of the people who elect us to serve. The statement of priority of these needs is the state budget, and while the details of my proposal will be explained later this month, the gravity of the problem – many years in the making – merits emphasis now.

Vermont has always taken pride in its reputation for balanced budgets, stubbornly adhered to as a top priority. This insistence on fiscal responsibility – despite being the only state in the union without a legal requirement for balance – has helped Vermont weather difficult financial times without resorting to drastic measures required of other states.

Only rarely, and always briefly throughout our history, has that insistence on financial integrity not prevailed. In those instances when it has not, the steps required to return the state to balance have always been less desirable than a steady allegiance to sustainability. Although our budget is not yet out of balance, it is clear that that allegiance to sustainability has been breached and must be restored immediately.

There are many areas of the budget that are growing at unsustainable rates, chief among them the Medicaid program. Nearly one in four Vermonters – compared to the national average of one in seven – now fall under the umbrella of this social welfare program originally designed specifically for the poor, infirm and disabled.

Today, we face at least a seventy million dollar deficit in Medicaid. Left unrestrained, the very next legislature, in the very next biennium, will confront a deficit of almost two hundred seventy million dollars – over a quarter of a billion dollars. That's an amount equivalent to twenty-five percent of our entire general fund budget. This deficit would be the largest in Vermont history. It threatens our fiscal stability, basic economic and health protections, and the already over-taxed Vermonter.

To eliminate a deficit of this magnitude, the legislature would have to impose draconian tax hikes on working people: raising personal income taxes by over fifty percent or nearly doubling the sales tax or almost quadrupling the gas tax.

These tax hikes would destroy the foundation of our economy. The fact is plain: we cannot, should not and must not tax our way out of this problem.

In the last biennium I proposed reforms that would have reduced this deficit and relieved its impact on other programs, but those reforms were rejected. Now, we do not have the luxury of time.

It falls on us – all of us – to find a solution that will save Medicaid for future generations before it collapses under the burden of its own weight. Getting spending under control will require leadership, and I am prepared to provide it. A solution will require a commitment as well from you, the legislature, to make those tough decisions required to put a responsible bill on my desk.

As you consider all of the other spending pressures you will surely face, including and especially additional health care spending, I ask you to tend to what we already have. I ask you to save Medicaid first.

And as we seek a balanced budget, it is important to acknowledge that we did not get in this situation because Vermonters are taxed too little; we're here because government has spent too much.

Already, Vermont's working families pay the 8th highest income tax rate in the nation and have the 12th highest burden of state and local taxes. And although we are making slow progress reducing the relative tax burden, it is still too high. Besides the heavy toll high taxes take on working families, a high tax environment also contributes to a business climate that makes job creation and economic prosperity more difficult.

During the past two years, we took many steps to improve Vermont's job environment. Our robust recovery has resulted in strong revenues that allowed us to replenish our rainy day funds and get Vermont on solid footing. This will make balancing the budget for the coming fiscal year easier than it would have been, but it would be a serious mistake to reverse this progress by raising taxes now.

I challenge this legislature to deliver to me a fiscally responsible, balanced budget that does not raise the tax burden on the people of our state.

The stakes are high, and the pressure exerted on us will be intense. As we work together for the benefit of all Vermont, special interests will fight fiercely. They will speak loudly, stage protests, and make dire predictions. But if we fail to stand firm, the eye of history will stare far more sternly on us than any special interest.

Within the constraints of a balanced budget there is little room for new spending programs. That is why I have proposed affordable health care reforms that will move us toward universal health insurance coverage, bringing peace of mind and security to thousands of uninsured Vermonters, while reducing the cost of health insurance for those who already have it, and employers who want to offer it to their workers.

Like saving Medicaid, health care reform is an issue that cannot tolerate delay. Vermonters' insurance premiums are swelling, prescription drug costs are rising, and small businesses and working families are having trouble affording the care they need. My plan for health care reform provides concrete steps to address these concerns.

The plan that I have offered is built around five fundamental principles to which any comprehensive plan must adhere. Real health care reform must lower the cost of care for those Vermonters who are struggling to keep up. Reform must be patient-centered and put decisions in the hands of patients and their doctors, not politicians and bureaucrats. Reform must increase choices and options of care. Reform must be affordable for Vermonters and sustainable for state government. And real reform must lower the cost of prescription drugs with initiatives at both the national and state levels.

As we begin this new biennium, let us demonstrate our bipartisanship by crafting together a drug reimportation bill that will not undermine our first-in-the-nation lawsuit against the FDA.

At the same time, we must be honest with the people of Vermont: drug reimportation is at best a short-term fix – perhaps short-lived – and will not be a viable option for many Vermonters. We must continue our fight for a national solution.

We must also recognize that prescription drugs are only one part of the soaring cost of health care. To fundamentally lower costs, we need to take more responsibility for our own health. That's why I will continue to push for innovative health care programs like the Chronic Care Initiative, Fit & Healthy Kids, and a Healthy Choices discount.

My plan for real health care reform is a starting point for this General Assembly. I know there will be other designs for new systems of care. I look forward to an open and honest debate about their merits and their value. But the final product must meet the fundamental principles I've set forth and cover all aspects of reform.

Vermonters cannot wait for another study, another year where premiums continue to rise and care moves out of reach. I ask this Legislature to act thoughtfully – but to act quickly – and deliver me a comprehensive and fiscally responsible health care reform package by adjournment this year.

As the pace of our economy's transition from a largely industrial base to a global information age quickens, we must continue our work to improve our infrastructure and empower Vermonters with the education and skills they need to excel in the next generation of jobs.

To keep our economy moving forward, we must keep goods, people, and ideas moving forward. Repairing roads and bridges, building critical transportation arteries, and expanding broadband and cell coverage must remain central to our job creation strategy.

We need to remain steadfast in our commitment to improve primary and secondary education, close the performance gaps, and encourage innovative approaches and technologies that improve student achievement.

Participants in today's – and more importantly, tomorrow's – economy must have opportunities to continue learning and upgrade their skills. We need to sustain our efforts to make our colleges more affordable by improving our support of higher education.

Everyone, young and old, must have access to the knowledge and skills to participate in the evolving economy. That is why I am proposing that we place an even greater emphasis on skills training so every working Vermonter can compete and succeed in the 21st Century.

Working together, we can educate and inspire a workforce that is second to none, making our working families more secure and our communities more prosperous.

Vermonters are known not for their wealth of riches, but for their richness of spirit. It is our strong-hearted independence and unforced kindness that defines us and our desire to make better that unites us.

Our urge to refine – to smooth the roughhewn and find natural symmetry – is elemental to the soul of Vermont. We carry it to our government – into school boards, town halls, committee rooms, and into these chambers – with the noble ambition to make the bad good and the good better.

It has brought us together today. As we consider the work before us, let us also consider how fortunate we are.

If, at the beginning, the Almighty gave to humanity a sliver of globe on which to carve a heaven on earth, it would be filled with verdant hills and sparkling lakes, open fields and forests thick with all His majesty. The joy of changing seasons would bless a people with a cycle of life and instill in them the spirit of freedom and a sense of unity.

And they would call it Vermont.

With a commitment to cooperation and common sense, we've put Vermont back on the path to prosperity. But there is much more for us to do and Vermonters expect, demand and deserve a government that will continue to work together.

And so it has come down to us: two chambers solidly Democrat, and one man loyally Republican, to come together in the spirit of civic virtue.

Guided by a common purpose, bound by a common history, with a genuine desire for cooperation, let us today begin the march toward our common destiny.

2006 State of the State
January 5, 2006

MR. PRESIDENT, MADAME Speaker, Members of the General Assembly, distinguished guests, fellow Vermonters:

Each time I rise to address this General Assembly, I stand humbled before you, before Vermont, before God. Vermonters have entrusted in us the privilege to serve them and, in their service, we have come to defend fairness, promote justice, and fight for progress.

We are drawn to this service in singular purpose: to give those without a place, a seat; to give those without a say, a voice; and to give those without a hope, a dream. We fight for Vermonters who live the old ways of having just enough, who ask for little, but who quietly struggle for a better tomorrow. The winters have not tempered their spirit – but forged within the mountainside of their souls the determination to push on.

It is within this spirit we draw our strength, our desire for relentless innovation, to replace the unacceptable, improve the inadequate, and better our best.

As Vermonters, we are proud of our great state: more Vermonters are working today than ever before and we have among the nation's lowest unemployment rates; our state has one of the greenest energy supplies in the country and our supply of renewable power is growing; Vermont was the first state to receive a "global commitment" waiver from the federal government to help save our Medicaid program; Vermont is one of the healthiest states in the union; we have one of the nation's lowest poverty rates; and, of course, our natural environment is unparalleled in its unspoiled beauty.

We have every reason to be proud of our state, but I know that Vermont can and must do even better. We must especially do better to make Vermont an affordable place to live, work and raise a family. We must recognize the burden imposed on Vermonters who are doing all they can just to get by as the state continues to ask of them more and more. We will strive to do better for them, and for their children and grandchildren, so that every generation might enjoy a lifetime of opportunity in our green hills.

The work we have undertaken these past three years has made Vermont a stronger, better state, and it is with an eye toward the future that I ask you to join me in the year to come to make it stronger still.

It is perhaps the men and women of the Vermont National Guard who today best illustrate the strength and resilience of Vermont. We've been fortunate in the last few weeks to welcome home hundreds of our loved ones, our friends and our neighbors who have returned from their deployments – but there are still many for whom we pray, including a member of this General Assembly, Representative Doran Metzger.

We support our troops unconditionally; their personal courage and conviction inspire every Vermonter and strengthen our call to serve the greater good.

With us today, representing all of the members of our armed forces as well as the state's veterans, and reminding us of the tremendous spirit, determination, and endurance of Vermont and its values, are members of the Vermont National Guard. Please join me in thanking them.

While the state of the state is strong, there is also unfinished business that requires our attention. We all agree that more can and should be done to improve access to health insurance. However, an equally pressing challenge is making health insurance more affordable for those who already have it.

The end of last session set in motion productive discussions around Vermont that allowed us to identify responsible, common sense reforms on which we all can agree. This year, I present these changes as part of a consensus reform package to be considered at the beginning of this session. I am grateful that this work has already begun in the Senate and I ask both chambers to pass this package and deliver it for my signature by the end of February.

We also need to work together to address the federal Medicare implementation challenges that are currently afflicting the entire nation. We must ensure that Vermont seniors have access to the prescription drugs they need at the price they were promised.

Earlier today, I directed the Agency of Human Services to immediately reinstate benefits to seniors who were previously enrolled in one of Vermont's prescription drug programs. This means that no senior who relied on state government for medicine will be turned away from a pharmacy. They will get the drugs they need and Vermont will continue to guarantee their affordability.

In addition, we will continue to press the federal government to quickly address these implementation challenges so seniors can take advantage of the federal prescription drug benefit program they were promised.

It is well documented that on the broader question of how best to extend health care coverage to all Vermonters and reduce insurance premiums there are a variety of opinions. Yesterday, the House dealt with the final vestiges of last year's health care debate. My hope is now that it is done, we can focus on the future, and what we can do together to provide real relief to Vermonters.

Two weeks ago, I presented a plan that will reduce health insurance costs, extend access to every resident, and offer Vermonters the same lower cost health insurance options available to consumers in other states. My plan increases Medicaid reimbursements to doctors to help reduce the need to shift costs onto the privately insured, and it does not require the government to make important medical decisions best left in the hands of doctors and patients. We can do this while staying within our means and without raising taxes.

In my plan, there is a role for government, but it is a role that complements rather than crowds out personalized care. It strengthens the safety net for the most vulnerable, without sacrificing the many benefits of a system that currently provides the highest quality health care in the world.

I hope to use the coming weeks to convince you that my plan for comprehensive health care reform is both bold and balanced, far-reaching and far-sighted.

And we must take a far-sighted approach. For two decades Vermont has pursued a course of greater government regulation of the health care system. Hindsight now allows us to assess the costs and benefits of such an approach.

The benefits are meaningful. Virtually every child has health insurance; our immunization rate is second highest in the nation; Vermont is consistently ranked near the top for prenatal care; we have one of the nation's lowest infant mortality rates; and we have taken important steps to provide mental health coverage to vulnerable Vermonters.

These policies have also had many unfortunate consequences, and after twenty years of gradually pursuing this approach, insurance premiums are higher than ever, the number of uninsured Vermonters is increasing and the government programs we already have are headed for bankruptcy. Even with Global Commitment, which allows us more time and flexibility to address the Medicaid cost crisis, the program is still headed for a five-year, $280 million deficit.

Currently, the program covers one in four Vermonters – the highest rate in the nation and nearly twice the national average. Managing the financial burden of Medicaid alone has proven a nearly impossible task requiring the state to take extraordinary steps, yet this crisis is still far from resolution. The notion of the state taking responsibility for managing the care of the other three-quarters of the population, as well-meaning as it may be, would result in dire consequences for Vermont's fiscal and economic health –not to mention the inevitable decline in health care quality that would occur once limited government budgets meet with unlimited consumer demands.

My health care reform plan accomplishes our shared goals without compromising quality care, and without biting off more than the taxpayer can chew. I ask the General Assembly to give my plan full consideration and a fair vote. Together, we can have real health care reform this year.

But health insurance is just one of the necessities of modern life where costs are quickly escalating beyond the average Vermont family's ability to afford them.

For many years, I have expressed a deep concern that Vermont is exporting too many of our youth. High taxes, a shortage of affordable homes, high energy costs, soaring school budgets and college tuitions, and a challenging economic environment all conspire to drive our young people to seek a more affordable life elsewhere, and prevent working-class Vermonters from getting ahead.

The stories are familiar:

Young people with college degrees forced to live with their parents for years after graduation because excessive college loans and high housing costs deny them the independence they had every right to expect by their early 20s.

The newlyweds who, despite two incomes, are confined to living in a small apartment – or even with their in-laws – because there are no starter homes available at a reasonable cost.

Years once spent building a nest egg for the future are instead spent subsidizing someone else's dream.

Grandparents who move out of state not just seeking warmer weather, but because they can't survive in Vermont on a fixed income when the cost of living escalates.

And perhaps the most familiar experience: parents who watch their children leave Vermont for college never to return permanently because the high cost of doing business in our state hinders the creation of the kinds of 21st century jobs they seek.

There is an increasing crisis of affordability and the signals are all around us – chiefly, the exodus of young people and new families, and the rapid graying of Vermont.

Vermont has the 6th highest cost of living in the nation, despite no major metropolitan areas. Already, the flight of young people as a result of high expense and limited opportunities has helped make Vermont the second-oldest state in the country.

Within twenty-five years the number of retirees will double while the number of working-age Vermonters will continue to shrink. In just the next decade there will be fifteen percent fewer Vermonters under the age of twenty than there were just five years ago.

For all the quality of life we enjoy, a lifetime in Vermont is becoming financially out of reach for middle and low-income residents, many of whom are native Vermonters whose families go back generations. The long-term cultural and economic consequences of this trend are significant and the threat to that famed quality of life is all too real.

I ask that as you consider legislation this session and in following sessions, put foremost in your thoughts the effects that legislation will have on the cost of living and doing business in Vermont. And I ask you to take substantive steps to bring some of the worst cost culprits under control.

We must take action now to adopt an agenda of affordability for Vermont's families. We need to begin today to remedy the high cost of health insurance; to address surging property taxes and housing costs that are squeezing working Vermonters; to help employers create more good-paying jobs; and to put a college education within reach of every Vermonter.

We must begin by recognizing that excessive taxation threatens our prosperity, reduces opportunity, and is an unjust burden on families. When government is consuming too much of its citizens' hard-earned dollars, it undermines and interferes with an individual's ability to prosper and discourages innovation and investments in job creation by employers.

Calvin Coolidge expressed well the philosophy that once defined his home state when he said, "I want the people of America to be able to work less for the government and more for themselves. I want them to have the rewards of their own industry. That is the chief meaning of freedom."

But too often, the sage advice of our native son has not been observed, and today Coolidge's Vermont has the nation's third highest tax burden as a percent of personal income.

This is one area where Vermont should not be proud to be a national leader.

If we are to make Vermont a more affordable state, the problem of over-taxation cannot be ignored and must not be exacerbated. Not too many years ago, we heard the impassioned promises that Act 60 would reduce property taxes. The forecasts portrayed a future of responsible and moderate growth, of sustainable spending spread equitably across all Vermont towns.

Tomorrow is now today and the reality is that education spending has grown at almost twice the rate of inflation, outstripped increases in the gross state product and far outpaced growth in the family checkbook. The average increase has been over 6% per year – nearly 60% overall growth since 1999.

Property tax burdens have multiplied to keep up with spending. Since 1999, property taxes have risen, on average, at a rate of almost 8% per year. Put another way, taxpayers will pay $407 million more in property taxes in 2007 than they paid in 1999 – a spike of nearly 82% in eight years. Even with the help of Act 68, if left unabated, the average tax bill will jump over 10% from just this year to next.

However, over the same period, enrollment in our schools has dropped 8%. We'll have over 8000 fewer students in September 2006 than we had in September 1999. When enrollment is dropping, but spending is rising and taxes are soaring, we have a problem that requires immediate action.

If we expect to keep Vermont affordable for Vermonters, we must act now to dramatically curb the unsustainable growth in property taxes. Today I am offering a comprehensive property tax relief plan for Vermont families to return sustainability to school spending, and give real power back to the local voters and school boards.

I am a firm believer in local control – but since Act 60 undermined that control, property taxes have spun out of control.

Some have offered a proposal to increase the state income tax to pay for education. Vermonters already pay some of the highest income taxes in the nation. Piling an education income tax on top of an already high income tax simply will not do for Vermont taxpayers. Moreover, raising the income tax does nothing to address the issue of higher spending.

As a matter of principle, taxes should not grow faster than your paycheck. So, I propose capping education property tax growth at no more than the rate of inflation each year. At roughly 3.5%, this target is sustainable and allows room for school budgets to grow responsibly to meet the needs of a community. If a town would like to spend more than the rate of inflation, my proposal will require a supermajority of 60% of the voters to pass the increase.

In addition, I propose a package of changes to restructure the income sensitivity program, including a measure to close loopholes in the prebate / rebate system – loopholes that allow owners of million-dollar homes to get five-figure prebate checks.

Combined with the return of the property tax surplus in the education fund, we will cut the statewide property tax rate by $.04 for all taxpayers. Further, with my relief plan, we can cut statewide rates by at least another $.10 in 2008 – that is almost $65 million in taxpayer savings in two years.

Act 60 eliminated the machinery and equipment property tax – giving businesses a property tax reduction on their fixed assets. However, because the key fixed asset of farmers is their land, our farmers could not enjoy this tax reduction. It is time to correct this double standard and repeal the education property tax on working farms by 2008.

This will save the average Vermont farmer more than $3,500 per year which can be put to good use maintaining farm equipment, barns and other facilities, as well as strengthening our agricultural community which is so important to us all.

Last year, this General Assembly added a provision into the final budget bill that I fear will lead to an unacceptable outcome: adding two more pre-kindergarten grades to the already stressed K-12 education system and putting taxpayers on the hook to fund it. Instead of this approach, we need to find ways to assist our private pre-school providers. Through Building Bright Futures, we must ensure that all our pre-schools are of high quality and that our children are safe. I am asking the General Assembly to reconsider the decision to further increase the cost of education and the growing tax bills that accompany those costs.

These measures to stem skyrocketing property taxes will keep more hard-earned money in the pockets of Vermonters – where it belongs.

Another factor driving the high cost of living in Vermont is housing. We must do more to ensure that every Vermonter has the ability to realize the American Dream.

Over the past five years, while the average household income has risen a respectable 3.7%, the median cost of a home surged 10% per year – almost triple the rate of income growth. Because of the growing disparity between housing prices and household income, the average Vermont homebuyer has substantially less purchasing power for housing than was the case just five years ago. Unless we address this problem now, the dream of owning a home in our state for the average Vermonter could slip away within a generation.

I want to work with this General Assembly – and with Vermont's strong network of housing providers – to address our shortage of low and middle-income housing. I believe that there are steps that we can take this year to move us forward, so let us pledge to work together and make affordable homes a long-term priority.

In addressing our housing needs, we must also recognize that Vermonters prize and cherish our historic downtowns and village centers, the traditional New England settlement patterns that make our communities such wonderful and unique places to live. I will propose to this legislature that we strengthen those communities – and establish an environment conducive to the creation of more homes and mixed-use development – with a new state designation called Opportunity Zones. Opportunity Zones will encourage municipalities to plan for their future needs, and will stimulate smart growth by streamlining permitting in those zones.

Our downtowns and our village centers are key to this state's continued economic growth and integral to our quality of life; we must do everything we can to help them prosper.

Not long ago I visited Vermont Precision Tools, a longtime manufacturer in Swanton. The company was founded in 1968 by Norm Leduc and Ray Boutin. The company manufactures precision tooling for a variety of sectors, including the industrial, automotive and medical industries. One of its products is this medical "burr" – a tiny surgical tool used for bone reconstruction in operating rooms worldwide.

In 2003, Vermont Precision Tools moved into a new, state-of-the art manufacturing facility in Swanton – staying close to their workforce and their roots. Over the last two years, the company has created twenty new jobs and it shows no signs of slowing. Because of its continuing innovation, its unwavering commitment to quality and the hard work of its skilled employees, Vermont Precision Tools has made its mark on this emerging global industry and its products are sold around the world.

The story of Vermont Precision Tools is a great Vermont story. It reminds us that the global economy is a reality that must be made into an opportunity; that we are not only competing with our neighbors, but with competitors half way around the globe; and it draws attention to the importance of higher education, workforce training and the role of science and technology in the 21st Century economy.

With the right combination of reforms and an intense focus on our future, we can build on the successes of the last three years and replicate this model anywhere in Vermont. That is why I am calling on this Legislature to join me in making Vermont a true leader in our national and global economy.

We must begin by creating a competitive advantage around vigorous and innovative economic sectors providing good-paying career opportunities in Vermont. This will encourage young Vermonters to stay and make a living here, and it will attract new talented individuals and employers to move to Vermont.

Ongoing global and national trends require that this economy – Vermont's new economy – be knowledge-based, and built around our history, culture, values and resources. It must be intertwined with our state's higher education enterprises and workforce development efforts, efforts that should be strengthened and expanded to ensure that all Vermonters have the tools they need to thrive in the economy of tomorrow. And it must recognize that the real engines of our economy are the small businesses and manufacturing companies that employ sixty-eight percent of all Vermonters.

Without this long-term vision – without this plan to recast the economic landscape and make Vermont affordable for Vermonters – our short-term successes will be fleeting. That is why today I present to you a plan to build generations of opportunity.

To create the next generation of jobs in Vermont, we must capitalize on our commitment to the natural environment. Protecting our land, air and water is not a partisan issue – it is a value that all Vermonters share. Vermont must leverage its incomparable commitment to the environment to become the Silicon Valley for environmental industries, or as Lieutenant Governor Dubie envisions, the Green Valley.

Vermont must become the international leader for marketable environmental products and the center of a global bazaar of environmental ideas. Vermont can become a leader in research and design, next generation manufacturing and export of environmentally related products.

This environmental focus will provide new opportunities at every level of the economy all across our state. Vermont businesses will need well-trained engineers and highly-skilled workers from Newport to Barre to Bennington to design and build these innovative products. As the companies prosper, the communities will flourish, and soon employees will need new homes, new cars and new services.

The Green Valley will need a sturdy infrastructure on which businesses can thrive. Good roads, strong bridges, and a telecommunications network that supports widespread cell phone coverage and broadband access are essential tools for any 21st century entrepreneur. To meet our ambitious telecommunications goals we will work proactively in partnership with private providers to expand capacity across the state.

A central issue in the affordability of Vermont is the need for economical and reliable sources of energy. The costs of heating your home or business and fueling your car or truck have risen dramatically in the last year. This year, the state has taken extraordinary measures to ensure home heating assistance for the most vulnerable over the winter. We must also aggressively safeguard consumers from price gouging and rate spikes that unfairly overcharge Vermonters.

Maintaining an affordable power supply requires a long-term strategic vision. Where we can, we must employ renewable energy sources and reduce demand by conserving more and promoting efficiency. The State has taken the lead on this by revamping our fleet system and instituting a plan to make state buildings environmentally friendly, and I have appointed a blue ribbon commission to recommend how we can extend these initiatives to the private sector.

But for consumers such as manufacturers, whose machines demand power to turn out their products, we must ensure competitively priced energy to help them keep and create good-paying jobs. In the coming years we will foster an affordable energy supply, rich in renewables, from both in-state sources and our neighbors in Canada. The need for reliable and reasonably priced power is fundamental for both employers and employees.

As we expand the need for a well-trained workforce, the nexus with higher education is critical. That's why I am proposing more substantial and direct investments in the University of Vermont, the Vermont State Colleges and the Vermont Student Assistance Corporation to fund innovative research, programs and equipment to support the sustainable technology sector.

Due to the advocacy of Senator Jeffords through the federal transportation bill, the University of Vermont has become one of the nation's ten National Transportation Research Centers, a designation that distinguishes UVM as a national leader in research and development and the center for an important new high tech and environmentally sustainable business cluster.

The Green Valley offers a quality place for workers to live, a strong environmental culture, and a great place to work, contribute to society, and raise their families. But the Green Valley will only succeed in attracting innovative 21st century businesses if we address the affordability of living and doing business in Vermont, including the cost of higher education.

Vermont has more colleges per capita than any other state. Still, sadly, Vermont leads the nation in the percentage of high school graduates who leave their state to go to college – and who, for the most part, will not make Vermont their home again in the course of their working lives.

And while we spend more per pupil on primary and secondary education than nearly any other state, our support of higher education is among the weakest.

The cornerstone of my effort to make college more affordable and keep Vermont's young people here is the Vermont Promise Scholarship program, a 15-year, nearly $175 million initiative.

The Vermont Promise Scholarship program will provide high school graduates more than 1,000 awards per year – over 12,000 scholarships during the life of the program – to attend one of the state's many outstanding institutions of higher education.

In return for the Vermont Promise Scholarship, we ask the graduates to start a life here in Vermont once they complete their studies. If they do, the state will forgive the full award; if they choose to chart their course elsewhere, the state will treat a portion of the scholarship as a loan.

This investment in scholarships for young Vermonters is made possible by using additional funds that will come to the state beginning in 2008 through the tobacco settlement agreement reached seven years ago. Vermont will receive one of the largest shares per capita because of our successful and aggressive stance against tobacco through litigation and legislation. As a result of our hard work to fight smoking, Vermont will be able to continue our cessation programs and fund our Vermont Promise Scholarship program.

By investing now in this generation of Vermonters, we are investing in our future leaders and problem solvers, and the source of our economic and cultural success in the years ahead. We are giving them important incentives to stay in Vermont to help us all build a better, brighter tomorrow. It is our promise to the next generation.

As we strive to bring generations of opportunity to all Vermonters, we must also keep our promise to ensure the safety of our communities; we cannot forget the most vulnerable Vermonters who depend on us for protection.

Last year, I asked the General Assembly to pass my multi-part "Safe Communities" legislation that would give parents and law enforcement officials new tools to keep Vermont families secure in their own neighborhoods.

Vermont is fortunate to be among the safest states in the nation. But today, there is a tiny population of hard-core criminals in our prison system who have not received treatment that might allow them to return to society and lead productive and nonviolent lives. These criminals are the worst of the worst: repeat rapists, child molesters, and murderers who, left untreated, represent a very high likelihood to reoffend once released.

Last month, I received a letter from a group of Winooski High School students who expressed their deep concerns about the recent release into their community of one such criminal with a long history of convictions for child molestation.

The letter read, in part: "We do not understand why someone with such a risk of assaulting young children, who refuses to have any psychiatric help, is being released into our community."

Frankly, I do not understand either. For the sake of our children and families, we must ensure that these extreme sexual and violent predators successfully complete treatment that will help prevent another victim before they are released into our neighborhoods among our children.

My civil confinement proposal should not be and does not need to be a partisan issue. Indeed, just across the lake in New York, leaders of the rival political parties have joined in support of a civil confinement proposal. I welcome and encourage bipartisan support for my Safe Communities legislation as well.

I do not want to come back next session with Vermont's children and parents still wondering why we have not acted. Today, once again, I ask this General Assembly to join me in support of this important change to keep untreated violent and sex offenders off our streets, out of our neighborhoods, far from our schools and away from our children.

To translate opportunity into achievement it must be joined with the hope for a better life. We must keep families and communities active and involved in bringing up young Vermonters so they might avoid the pitfalls that lead to a life of crime or perpetuate the cycle of dependence. I want every child to have a healthy relationship with a supportive adult, to feel valued at home and in his or her community and to contribute to our state's future.

Helping kids stay drug-free is the first step. While we've made progress in recent years in drug enforcement, education and treatment, we must continue to expand our efforts to combat substance abuse in Vermont.

Mentoring is another way to help teach our children Vermont values. I am proposing a strategic initiative called "Vermont Mentors!" to significantly expand mentoring throughout our state.

And for Vermont's foster children, those kids transitioning from the care of the state to adulthood, we must pledge the support, the tools and the guidance they need to achieve their dreams. The state must be by their side, not in their way, as they cut their own path toward independence.

Late last summer, we saw the strength and spirit of the Vermont community in full bloom. Just days after our nation's worst natural disaster, Vermonters were quick to respond, and this small and mighty state was among the very first to reach out to our fellow Americans and deliver lifesaving supplies.

The aid came in many forms. As Dorothy and I visited collection sites around the state, the tremendous outpouring by so many Vermonters touched us deeply. We met a woman in Montpelier who, while volunteering on the State House lawn, had her shoes packed up by accident and loaded into a truck. Her response was simply, "There's someone in Mississippi who needs those shoes more than I do." Together, in an overwhelming showing of generosity and selflessness, Vermonters worked to donate, package, load and deliver sixty-five tractor-trailer trucks jammed with supplies – more than four million pounds of material to the devastated Gulf Coast.

Among the truckers and troopers who transported the goods was Buck Adams, an independent hauler out of Bellows Falls. Buck, an excavator by trade, was quick to call and give his time to make the run south. He traveled to Mississippi in his own cramped short-haul tractor, forfeiting a week's wages to make the round trip. Despite these difficulties, Buck was ready to volunteer for a second assignment.

In addition to relief convoys, Vermont coordinated state assets such as National Guard resources, public health officers, medical personnel, and hazardous material teams that were deployed to the affected region. In this group were thirteen local rescue departments who answered the call for ambulances following Hurricane Rita. The volunteer drivers convoyed south and spent thirty days helping sort through the aftermath in Houston.

Another group – Vermont firefighters – traveled to the Gulf Coast to offer community counseling and outreach for the neediest victims.

There were countless other individual efforts that didn't make the front page of the papers, just anonymous generosity to people in desperate need.

One story I heard was about a sixth grader named Erin Reiner from St. Johnsbury. Erin's pastor gave her some seed money and told her to put it to good use for others. Erin took it upon herself to sew 200 scarves by hand. She sold each and every scarf for $5 and donated all the money – $1000 – to the American Red Cross Hurricane Relief fund. A remarkable effort.

Vermont's generosity for the hurricane victims didn't require government; government simply provided the vehicle and Vermonters did all the rest. This is the true spirit of Vermont community – always ready to come together across any boundary to help a neighbor in need.

Both Buck and Erin embody Vermont community, ingenuity, sacrifice and service. They join us in the balcony today and I want to thank them – and I want to thank every Vermonter who donated time, money, food or clothes – for their service to our fellow Americans. You make Vermont very proud.

Today, I have asked for your cooperation addressing some of Vermont's greatest challenges.

Let us carry forward the strength of our forbears and the spirit of our community to push beyond the everyday boundaries that too often preclude progress.

Let us advance an agenda of affordability for all Vermonters so that this generation and all those that follow may enjoy the blessings of our magnificent state and the promise of Vermont.

Let us strengthen our communities and keep them safe for the young and the young at heart.

And let us harness the value and the momentum of every success and move forward to a truly prosperous Vermont.

As I look ahead, I'm increasingly optimistic. My vision for Vermont remains, at its core, one of hope and opportunity. I envision a state, as all of you do, where the opportunity to prosper is universally accessible and where this prosperity grows stronger with each generation.

Thank you, and may God bless America and our great state of Vermont.

Third Inaugural Address
January 4, 2007

Mr. President, Madame Speaker, distinguished guests, my fellow Vermonters:

Fifty years ago, on this same Thursday, Robert Stafford presided, as Lieutenant Governor, over a joint assembly as Vermont's officers took their oaths and Governor Joseph Johnson delivered his inaugural address.

Two years later, Governor Stafford would deliver his own inaugural and note that, "There can be but one ultimate aim for all of us. It is to take the necessary action today to make Vermont a better place in which to live in every spiritual, social and economic sense for ourselves and our children."

This unadorned, ageless declaration explains succinctly the deep inspiration within him and reminds us today of our own responsibilities.

Ladies and gentlemen, please join me in honoring the extraordinary life of Robert T. Stafford.

I have had, on three occasions now, the privilege of placing my hand upon our family bible and pledging, on my sacred honor, to faithfully execute the responsibilities of governor.

Our oaths are taken, according to our customs and traditions, in public ceremony – symbolizing the covenant into which we have entered. We solemnize, through our words, a relationship that has at its core the noble virtue of trust.

Here today bearing witness to this convention are members of our National Guard. These extraordinary men and women represent all of those individuals, and their families, who protect and defend the world's most dignified expression of self-governance. They are here today to remind us of our proud past, the challenges of the present and our obligations for the future. Please join me in thanking them and all of the men and women of our armed forces.

For a second biennium the people of Vermont elected the highest constitutional officers of one party, and a Legislature controlled by another. Appreciating the progress we made in the last session, they have no doubt concluded that such a balance serves Vermont well. Vermonters aren't interested in partisan intrigue – they are interested in results.

Over the last several years, we've taken major steps to ensure each new generation of Vermonters enjoys greater prosperity and peace of mind.

We began construction of this new, more secure, economic framework by first articulating our economic development ethics – values that guide all levels of our policymaking. We rejected the notion that jobs come at the expense of the environment, and that environmental protection must be compromised to have economic progress, stating without equivocation that we must have both. This third way – The Vermont Way – is committed to both our environment and our economy.

We then took aggressive action to address our immediate economic future, made major commitments to putting Vermonters back to work, and reversed Vermont's image as a place unfriendly to job creation by passing the state's largest jobs package and following the path outlined in my Plan for Prosperity.

We renewed our commitment to Vermont's hardworking taxpayers by passing only balanced budgets. Vermonters expect us to be fiscally responsible and live within our means. The budget I present to you for the coming fiscal year will once again be in full balance and reflect the priorities of the people of our state.

Finally, by focusing on affordability – on those issues most affecting working Vermonters – we've identified the means to address our changing population and make our state more affordable and its families more prosperous.

Moderating the cost of living is a prerequisite to achieving the prosperity and peace of mind within our reach. That is why full implementation of the Affordability Agenda remains an essential priority, and we should begin by following through on our commitment to making higher education more affordable.

Our system of higher education must be a centerpiece of our economy, producing the innovators whom we need to compete and succeed in the 21st Century. We are a step closer to our goals thanks in large part to the Legislature's recognition of the problem and the hard work of our Next Generation Commission. The Commission has made some excellent recommendations and I thank them for their inclusive, diligent effort.

Our task now is to build on these recommendations and launch a comprehensive package of Next Generation initiatives this year.

We must fully implement Catamount Health, reforms already regarded as the most far-reaching of their kind anywhere in the country. This will require flexibility and a continued commitment to our common goals, but I'm confident that we can make these landmark health care reforms a resounding success.

Catamount Health will change the lives of thousands of Vermonters by insuring the uninsured and offering affordable premiums to those who otherwise couldn't purchase their own insurance. Together, we faced the health care challenge head on, we put Vermonters ahead of politics and delivered on our promise, and for that we can all be proud.

We must do more to put homeownership within reach of every Vermonter. That is why I propose the New Neighborhoods Initiative to facilitate home construction through a process that is predictable and less costly.

Young people entering the workforce need homes that are safe and affordable. Growing families ascending the economic ladder deserve the peace of mind and convenience of a welcoming neighborhood near where they work and where their children go to school. And the recruitment of skilled employees should not be impeded by the lack of affordable homes.

Vermonters take pride in the work that we do; from educators to excavators, we wake each morning with the same determination to do our best to provide for our families. In this biennium, we must send a strong message to Vermonters that hard work matters and that we will not take more than is necessary to run state government and fund our schools.

The oppressive property tax burden is the single greatest threat to Vermonters' renowned resolve. Property taxes continue to increase at more than double the rate of inflation – and growth in the family checkbook – at a time when the number of students in our classrooms is declining. We must work together to ease the weight of property taxes on working Vermonters – without shifting it to another tax. To do that, we must cap property taxes.

Dorothy and I are proud to have sent our boys to public school where they received a quality education. I believe we can cap property taxes without compromising the quality and success of our public schools. We can continue to increase our investment in these important institutions – but at a rate that Vermonters can afford.

I have met with Speaker Symington and Senator Shumlin and, while our approaches may differ, we agree the real culprit is unsustainable increases in spending. Like our health care reform efforts, we need to work together, explore all options and focus on containing costs, not on raising taxes.

Vermont already has one of the highest income tax rates and per capita tax burdens in the country. Raising taxes to pay for education would intensify the problem, not solve it. Raising taxes would be unfair to working Vermonters, discourage innovation and threaten economic growth.

Making Vermont affordable is imperative. Keeping our families safe is equally important. Two weeks ago, I was proud to stand with Barre Mayor Thom Lauzon after the recent crackdown on drug activity in his city. Mayor Lauzon's determination to hold drug dealers accountable is a model we have seen work in other cities, like Rutland.

Working through the Vermont Drug Task Force, we look forward to continuing our efforts in communities where the state can be a partner for change.

In Vermont, we are fortunate to have a strong community of law enforcement, firefighters, and emergency medical workers. Whether volunteer or career, they have committed their lives to public service and, in turn, let us continue our clear commitment to them. Please join me in thanking Vermont's first responders for their hard work and dedication.

Over the past four years, first with the Plan for Prosperity, now with the Affordability Agenda, we have made steady, substantive progress on the most difficult and complex issues facing Vermont families. While we must still address many pressing challenges swiftly and in this session, we are now ready to look forward – ahead of today's affairs – to shape a future for Vermont that ensures our prosperity for decades to come.

All of the steps we've taken are part of a larger vision that has brought us to the early edge of tomorrow, to the threshold of a renaissance that will – if we take care to see it through – produce the greatest economic advancements of our time.

Vermont has a legacy of leadership that stretches back to the state's founding. We will take that heritage forward and become a leader in a new economic frontier – a system of continual and substantial growth that harnesses our immeasurable intellectual wealth. To do so, we must bring together advancements in technology and education around the core of our shared environmental ethic. We must join the best of our past with a resurgence of Vermont's well-known resourcefulness and inventiveness.

Our future is the very definition of Yankee ingenuity and is rooted firmly in our traditions. A founding tenet of Vermont is creative adaptation – turning sap into syrup and selling it as gold – and our future will be built on that principle.

Our approach will combine Vermont's unparalleled environmental values with innovations in education and a telecommunications infrastructure superior to that found in the most modern cities. I call this approach "The Vermont Way Forward" and it will position Vermont squarely ahead of forces driving the global economy. The Vermont Way Forward advances our traditional industries through pioneering approaches to rural development. It protects our forests and fields for time-honored uses and applies scientific innovation to speed the clean up of our lakes and streams. And it strengthens Vermont's agrarian roots with technology that allows farmers to grow locally but compete globally.

Our approach embraces our cherished natural environment beyond its bountiful material resources and focuses our industry on one of the greatest engineering challenges of this century: finding practical environmental solutions that balance growth and resources around the world.

We will weave into our economy companies that share our sensible approach to protecting the environment. We will cultivate innovators in environmental engineering and become the center for the solutions of tomorrow, building on Lieutenant Governor Dubie's vision of a Green Valley.

The Vermont Way Forward will be built by Vermonters and emerge from markets that demand it; but, as a state, we must assemble the foundation from which it will prosper.

Today, I present the primary elements of the Vermont Way Forward – a four-part strategy of environmental leadership, job creation, technological advancement and innovative education – a strategy that will allow Vermont the opportunity to complete an economic transformation that no state has achieved, but all will envy.

The Vermont Way Forward begins by reaffirming the importance of our natural environment and our commitment to a balanced approach.

Overall, Vermont's global environmental footprint is quite light. We have developed a responsible and growing portfolio of renewable energy sources. We currently capture more greenhouse gas than we produce. We were the first state to sign on to the Regional Greenhouse Gas Initiative, and my administration adopted tougher rules mandating California Emissions Standards for cars and trucks.

Vermont has joined the 25 x '25 alliance to advance renewable energy solutions with the goal to produce 25% of our energy from renewable sources by 2025. And state government is a leader in reducing greenhouse gases through my Comprehensive Environmental & Resource Management program.

We have made enormous progress, but motor vehicles still account for 45% of greenhouse gas emissions in Vermont. To reduce emissions, lead us toward energy independence and expand the market for environmentally preferable fuels, I offer four proposals:

First, I ask that you approve a percentage point reduction of the tax on fuel-efficient and hybrid vehicles and reward Vermonters for making environmentally friendly choices. I request that you support a tax rate reduction on bio-diesel for individuals and businesses that use it for transportation purposes, so we can cultivate the commercial market for bio-fuels. I seek your support for a tax incentive that will make bio-fuels as affordable as regular home heating oil. And lastly, I hope that you'll support the effort I am making to substantially increase the use of alternative fuels in state government – both in our vehicles and our buildings – so that we remain a leader in this important transition.

These are important steps, but our efforts to reduce the effects of greenhouse gases and other pollutants must now go far beyond the leadership we provide through our example.

By attacking the prime drivers of greenhouse gas emissions and redoubling our pledge to use renewable energy resources, Vermont will do even more to strengthen its position as a world leader in the environmental sciences.

If we are to have a truly meaningful impact on global environmental issues, we must lead the world in developing environmental solutions, and market those solutions to companies, states and countries who can only covet Vermont's deeply imbued environmental ethic.

The second part of the Vermont Way Forward is an aggressive job creation strategy that will retain existing employers, retrain current employees and work to recruit firms that specialize in the growing field of environmental engineering, and the development of related products and services.

Environmental engineering is a discipline that identifies and implements solutions to problems such as air pollution, storm and wastewater management, hazardous materials and water supply contamination. The global demand for these services is large and growing, especially in emerging industrial nations. Many of these countries, such as China, are just now recognizing the effect of rampant growth and are beginning to develop and implement strategies to address prior and future impacts, and, in turn, are looking for environmental solutions.

Environmental engineering is Vermont's next captive industry and we have the foundation from which the sector can flourish.

The state will marshal public and private resources to grow this portion of our economy. To help guide this work, I will create through Executive Order an Environmental Engineering Advisory Council comprised of Vermonters with expertise in engineering, math, science and technology and appointed by both the administration and the Legislature.

This effort will leverage the innovation and knowledge of Vermonters to create a major new industry dedicated to resolving the most complex environmental challenges of our time. Our obligation now is to be sure the infrastructure exists to complete this economic transformation.

There is no doubt that a safe and reliable system of roads and bridges is essential for today's economy, but the critical infrastructure for the future of Vermont will not much look like a car, a culvert or a bend in the road. It will look like this.

In my hand there is wireless mobility, complete access and clear connections. In my hand is fairness and equity for all of Vermont. In my hand is both freedom and unity.

In three years, this phone will be capable of downloading email, images and video at speeds faster than most home broadband today. It will allow Vermonters to work from anywhere, anytime, unimpeded by spotty coverage, bad connections and the constant aggravation of dropped calls.

We've made great strides in improving cellular coverage along main corridors, but large areas of Vermont still have no signal. Although in the last three years we've helped over 45,000 more homes and offices get access to broadband internet – so nearly 90% of Vermont homes have access – the remaining 10% will take many more years to reach by traditional means.

While we take incremental steps to build a hard-wired network, the wireless world moves ahead. Homes that do not have broadband available are becoming increasingly difficult to sell. Entrepreneurs looking to start a new business will barely consider breaking ground in a community without good cellular coverage. Broadband internet and wireless cellular are no longer mere conveniences afforded to urbanites or the well-heeled; they are a fundamental part of modern life for all Vermonters, as essential as electricity and good roads. This is the technological foundation of the Vermont Way Forward.

Thanks to the work we've done, Vermont is well positioned to leap over existing technology and support both broadband and cellular communications for the entire state.

Wireless communications and broadband internet access are near the point of convergence – meaning the technologies that support each will be the same. More specifically, modern telecommunications will be based on Internet Protocol, or IP, a digital language that can support voice calls – like cell phones and standard telephones – as well as internet communications – such as email and web pages.

Building on these technological advances, I propose that by 2010, Vermont be the nation's first true "e-state" – the first state to provide universal cellular and broadband coverage everywhere and anywhere within its borders. When you turn on your laptop, you're connected. When you hit the send button on your cell phone, the call goes through. There would be no more endless downloads, no more hopeless hellos, and no more "can you hear me now."

This goal is within our grasp if we move quickly and decisively during this legislative session. To facilitate the creation of our "e-state," I propose a Vermont Telecommunications Authority that will partner with private enterprise to build a next generation infrastructure that supports universal broadband and cellular coverage. The state will back $40 million of bonding by the Authority, which will leverage more than $200 million in private investment. The Authority will serve as a bridge between public sector efforts and private sector investments and will seek to complement – not replace – the role of service providers and infrastructure developers.

Unlike building more roads or bigger buildings to support growth, the commercial infrastructure of tomorrow will be almost invisible, but for a handful of towers and antennas.

To support the work of the Authority, we need to reduce the time it takes to build a truly modern infrastructure. I will be proposing a series of responsible modifications to Vermont's permitting laws that will balance our environmental values with the need to move rapidly. Those measures will include using state-owned structures and rights-of-way to speed required construction.

The benefits of an "e-state" are evident to current and prospective employers. It represents meaningful connections within Vermont and with the vast world outside. Whether it means a construction worker can receive a business call at a remote job site, a bed and breakfast can offer guests wireless cellular and broadband, a feed store can order new inventory online or a small mail-order business can cut calling costs, our "e-state" strategy establishes the platform for success across all sectors of the economy.

The advantages of a state-of-the-art telecommunications platform extend well beyond the economic value of the Vermont Way Forward. A true "e-state" enhances our public safety network, extends the reach of health care, and improves the education of young Vermonters.

Ever-present cellular coverage will give residents and visitors an extra measure of protection and provide a communications network where police officers of one town can talk to firefighters of another.

The emergence of telemedicine, made possible by our universal broadband network, will offer dramatically enhanced monitoring services to chronically ill patients and the elderly. Vermonters with chronic conditions will be able to transmit information instantly to their doctors who can respond to anomalies or alarming trends.

Vermont is fast becoming a leader in health care innovation, led by Catamount Health and the Blueprint for Health. While our best-in-the-nation broadband network can never replace the compassionate touch of our health care providers, it will make available to them the most modern tools to improve quality and reduce costs.

The education of our children is the single most important and lasting impact of our "e-state" initiative. Affordable broadband services provide every child with access to the educational resources of the best schools and libraries throughout the world, as well as offering continuing education opportunities for lifelong learners.

Teachers and students would have at their fingertips a world's worth of educational resources. Whether it's online classes, tutorials to supplement classroom learning or internet video links with other classrooms throughout the world, our network will firmly establish Vermont as the best place to live and raise a family.

Our strong commitment to education will not stop there. Vermonters have always prized a quality education, but global competition demands an even higher level of aptitude from graduating students. We cannot simply put more money into the same system and expect better results. We have to look at the system with fresh eyes and rethink how to provide all students a chance to reach their full potential.

Senator Stafford understood that to give students a chance at success was to open up the world to them. Among his many accomplishments is the college loan program that bears his name. This unprecedented level of financial support has sent generations of kids to college.

We have now our own opportunity to help generations of young Vermonters obtain the skills they need to succeed in this century – and ensure they are learning math, science, technology and engineering as well as, or better, than their counterparts throughout the world. That is why I am proposing the creation of Robert T. Stafford Schools for Math, Science and Technology. These regional Stafford Schools for high school students will go beyond the scope of today's technical education and emphasize the skills needed for the next wave of scientific advancements.

The education of our children is important to all of us and I want to work with the Legislature to raise the quality of our educational system in creative ways. To this end, I propose to continue the good work of the Next Generation Commission and ask you to extend its charter to study the creation of Stafford Schools and other means to bring math and science competency to new levels.

The Vermont Way Forward is a model that takes our economy in a bold new direction. It empowers our balanced, practical environmental values and leverages them into new, good-paying jobs. It directs our educational system to teach tomorrow's leaders the skills they need to compete in the global economy. And it revolutionizes our telecommunications infrastructure by making Vermont the nation's first "e-state" where quality cell coverage and broadband internet are available to every Vermonter anywhere, anytime.

We have available to us the resources to secure for the benefit of generations of young Vermonters the opportunities and prosperity ahead. We have the opportunity to build an economy that favors the development of intellectual resources; an economy that embraces our old ways, and encourages their advancement through new means; an economy that ensures the security of every family and provides all Vermonters with the chance to enjoy our unparalleled quality of life without worrying that the costs of living here will exceed what they receive in their next paycheck.

The Vermont Way Forward captures these aspirations and embodies the best of Vermont.

You see this promise in the hands and faces of every Vermonter. As I have traveled Vermont, these hands and faces have instilled in me a new sense of purpose for the future of our great state.

I have shaken the hard-calloused hand of a hill farmer and in his leather-faced smile seen the hope of spring. I have warmed the thin hands of older Vermonters, their eyes still sparkling between deep gray granite lines of age.

I have touched the shoulder of a proud father hoisting his daughter heavenward; the warm blanket of a mother wrapped in the embrace of her newborn son.

And I have held the tender hands of young Vermonters, their shining eyes illuminating the path to tomorrow – blind to our differences, but bound to our promise to make this world better for them.

Now, in our hands, Vermonters have placed their optimism for this century. In our faces, they seek honesty, integrity and our commitment to a common purpose. And for them, we shall deliver.

When we clasp hands at the end of this biennium, let it be in celebration of our shared accomplishments for all Vermonters. Let our eyes be alight with progress. And let our actions speak boldly to the generations that lie before us.

2008 State of the State
January 10, 2008

Mr. President, Madam Speaker, Members of the General Assembly, my fellow Vermonters:

As 2008 opens, the hope of a new year – of a new beginning – unfolds before us, touching the horizon of a new generation. For centuries, our people have been held by a faith in tomorrow, by the glory of God's gift: the promise of Vermont.

As public servants, we are stewards of this promise, a responsibility we bind with an oath, and why we have gathered in the people's house today. I welcome you back to Montpelier and offer my sincere wish that we may work together with the shared duty of improving the lives of our fellow Vermonters.

We strive to share the virtues of our forbearers, those values of hard work, honesty, courage and sacrifice. There is no finer group of Vermonters who exemplify and embody those qualities than the men and women who defend our freedoms and protect our homes and neighborhoods. They are guardians of liberty, keepers of security and their uncommon sacrifice must never go unappreciated. Please join me in thanking the men and women of the Vermont National Guard, and soldiers, sailors, airmen and Marines who serve our nation both here and abroad – as well as Vermont's first response community – our firefighters, police officers and emergency workers.

In the 231 years since state government first met, we have faced many trials that have tested the mettle of Vermont values. Through natural disasters, national recessions, financial hardship and wars fought on American soil and foreign sands, we have emerged from each crucible with our will unbroken and our spirit strengthened. Our buoyant spirit is why, when we work together, guided by common purpose, Vermont works and works well.

But my chief concern is that Vermonters are working harder than ever to make ends meet. As we convene for this second half of the biennium, families in our state confront issues of affordability – challenges that moms and dads and grandparents must grapple with day-to-day. With health care premiums increasing by double digits, fuel topping three dollars per gallon, and property taxes continuing a steady climb, families are feeling the squeeze. Compounding these challenges, homeownership remains out of reach for too many Vermonters. These are the principal barriers to prosperity and the fundamental issues that this General Assembly must confront and make progress on this year.

While we remain diligent and focused on our key priorities, we must not ignore other important issues like climate change – indeed we would do so at the peril of our cherished environment.

And with all challenges we face, we must keep our vision far-reaching, but our goals practical, achievable and affordable.

With support from the Legislature, we have made significant progress to improve the lives of our fellow Vermonters. We passed the largest jobs package in our state's history and streamlined our permit process. We helped a new generation realize the dream of higher education with college scholarships and invested millions in skills training for working men and women. And we are moving forward with the e-State initiative – a plan to make Vermont the first state with high-speed internet and cell phone coverage available everywhere within our borders by the end of 2010.

As a result of our steadfast focus on economic growth, in the last five years, we've created 12,000 new jobs and our unemployment rate remains well below the national average.

I was proud to work with many of you to pass the Health Care Affordability Act. These reforms are a national model and will help to contain costs and ensure coverage for those who previously could not afford it. They are an example of what we can accomplish when we put progress ahead of partisanship.

We've provided seniors the option of staying home as they age, through our first-in the nation Choices for Care program. Dorothy and I know firsthand the challenge of caring for aging parents and how important it is to her mother to have the option of remaining at home now that she is no longer able to care for herself. Every Vermonter deserves that choice.

We can be particularly proud of the fact that Vermont has the highest percentage of its children insured. Right now we're engaged in a fight to protect these children – and others across the country – from partisanship in Washington that threatens to undo what Vermont has done. Vermonters can be certain of this: I will continue to insist that Washington live up to its obligations to our children.

We've accomplished these successes – and many others – with steady financial leadership and by holding the line on taxes. Vermont is not a large state with deep pockets. We have managed our finances prudently. We have balanced expanding needs with limited resources and done so with compassion and fairness. For this vigilance, Vermont has earned the highest possible bond rating – the best among New England states.

Still, I remain mindful of the turbulence and uncertainty in the national economy and will watch closely any developments here at home that may impact Vermont's sound financial position.

This common sense approach has laid the secure foundation upon which we start building today. Indeed, it is the very reason I can report that the state of our State stands strong.

Now, with one eye to the future, and one on the bottom line, we must strike the right balance of protecting key government services while making smart investments for the years ahead.

This will require that we be innovative, rethinking business as usual at every level, revitalizing what works well and reforming what must work better. We must seek efficiencies while strengthening services; stretch resources while protecting the most vulnerable; and treat precious taxpayer dollars as if we earned them ourselves.

Today, I lay out a series of proposals to achieve prosperity through affordability and to rethink, revitalize and reform the way our state approaches its most pressing challenges.

By making health care, homeownership and the tax burden more affordable – and by making investments in job creation and our natural environment – our families and our state will prosper.

The cost of health care remains a barrier to prosperity and the peace of mind our families deserve.

We should begin by acknowledging the great progress we have made and build on it. There were over 35 different initiatives within the Health Care Affordability Act – all designed to improve access, and the quality of the care we receive.

We are off to a great beginning with the new Catamount Health Plans and premium assistance programs. In just three and a half months, more than 1700 previously uninsured Vermonters have health insurance and 2500 more are in the process of enrolling. Now, they can get the care they need, when they need it, and without fear of not being able to afford it.

Even with these achievements, we need to keep moving ahead with responsible reforms to reduce the cost of insurance for families and small businesses.

The platform for meaningful progress on health care is the report of the bipartisan Health Care Reform Commission. There are a number of areas where we agree and should act quickly.

We agree that we should eliminate the technicality allowing insurance companies to deny coverage for small businesses with fewer than 75% of employees under the employer's plan. This provision hurts both employers and employees who are stranded without insurance and puts additional strain on government-sponsored programs.

We agree we can provide coverage to more young adults by allowing parents to keep them on their family plans longer. We agree a reinsurance mechanism can lower the cost of insurance. This is an idea I've advocated in the past. Any such proposal should neither require employers to drop their existing insurance nor establish a new and complex government program.

We agree we must enhance our focus on chronic conditions, including obesity – a preventable factor in increasing health care costs that must be addressed. With your support, we can place a prevention specialist in each region of our state and provide resources to encourage more community-based health initiatives.

We also agree that health information technology can improve quality and reduce costs. I ask that you support my plan to help primary care physicians acquire electronic health information systems, with the goal that every doctor in Vermont will be using them by the end of 2010.

With so much common ground among us, so many areas of agreement – and the financial security of so many families at stake – we must make more progress this year. I therefore request that this Legislature make affordable health care the top priority and send me a bill before Town Meeting.

Vermonters have a right to feel safe in their homes and neighborhoods. While we live in one of the safest states in the country, we continue to confront criminals who tear at the fabric of our communities.

Working with victim advocates and others, we've formed alliances against domestic violence, drug abuse and sex crimes. It is my hope that this year we will strengthen the special units that investigate these crimes and pass legislation that invests in domestic violence prevention.

Further, as we confront the scourge of substance abuse, I ask you to once again make prevention and enforcement the strategy of choice by investing in DETER – my Drug Education, Treatment, Enforcement and Rehabilitation program. We must continue to send a clear message to drug pushers and violent criminals that they have no place in our homes – no place in our communities – no place anywhere in our state.

Building safe and affordable communities across our state to meet the growing demand for housing is critical to the success and prosperity of all Vermonters. Affordable homes are important economic assets for growing families. They provide peace of mind for those who want to live near their job and their children's school. And affordable homes are an important recruiting tool for employers.

The average cost of a home has nearly doubled in the last ten years. Today, there are about 30,000 Vermont households who have outgrown their current space, but are unable to move up because of price and availability. To address this pressing challenge, we must support policies that encourage the construction of homes working Vermonters can afford. New home construction has the added benefit of stimulating economic growth and creating jobs.

I propose a revitalized New Neighborhoods initiative that streamlines our regulatory systems, creates incentives for communities and complements the existing housing production network. Revised provisions of this initiative address concerns I heard from this Legislature last year.

One exciting component of this initiative is my Urban Homesteading proposal. Throughout Vermont's downtowns there are buildings with thriving street level commercial space and retail shops but vacant or underutilized space on the upper floors. My proposal creates tax incentives to encourage first-time homeowners to invest in these spaces – increasing the availability of affordable homes and spurring economic growth in our downtowns and village centers.

The demand for more affordable homes all across our state is real. We can no longer afford inaction – now is the time to put the dream of homeownership within reach of every family.

It is not only the cost of purchasing a home that Vermonters struggle with, but also the cost of owning a home.

Last year we enacted meaningful reforms to ease steep yearly increases in property tax bills by calling for voters to consider an alternative budget for school districts that propose spending increases beyond a certain level. This mechanism will help make our increasing investment in education sustainable.

While we wait for this commonsense cap on property tax increases to take effect, we must create a bridge to stabilize tax bills right away. That's why I propose we provide more immediate property tax relief – Vermont families need help today.

We can cut property taxes directly by $25 million and invest another $25 million in school modernization projects by utilizing the projected $50 million of proceeds from leasing our state lottery. Not only will this proposal ease the financial strain on homeowners, it will help clear the backlog of school construction, giving our students 21st century learning environments in energy efficient buildings, which will save taxpayers money in the long run.

I recognize that my proposal to lease the state lottery is generating much discussion but the need for property tax relief is acute and taxpayers expect us to find ways to optimize state government and return those savings to them. I encourage you to keep an open mind, carefully weigh the advantages of this proposal and make your decision based on the pressing needs of property taxpayers.

Vermonters are always willing to pay their fair share for public safety, roads, education and programs for the disadvantaged, but – any way you study it – the tax burden is very high and people need relief. This is why I will continue to resist calls to raise the income tax, payroll tax, property transfer tax, home heating fuel tax, gas tax and other taxes.

We must continuously rethink how best to achieve equity in our tax system, because unfair or excessive taxation threatens prosperity and stifles innovation.

In 2004, we closed a loophole in our corporate tax policy that benefited large out-of-state corporations to the competitive disadvantage of homegrown, Vermont-based employers. By closing this loophole we were able to reduce the tax burden for our employers. In 2005, our top rate was 5th highest in the nation. After lowering the rate, and reducing the burden by 10.5%, we're now ranked 17th in the nation – making Vermont a more attractive place to start and grow a business.

Today, I am proposing to close another tax loophole – one that penalizes working Vermonters.

Our current tax structure taxes earned income – that is, your hourly wage or salary – at a higher rate than it taxes unearned income. What this means is that a working man or woman in Vermont making $50,000 a year pays nearly 50 percent more tax than someone who does not work and simply lives off investment or trust fund capital gains income in the same amount.

Our state is one of only a few that has such an unfair penalty for doing an honest day's work. This is grossly unfair. We must close this loophole and eliminate this working tax penalty.

We all know that Vermont's income tax rates are among the highest in the nation. By making these changes, we can substantially lower tax rates for middle class working Vermonters. We will also lower our top rate – which is the highest in the country – to increase our competitive advantage when recruiting employers to start or expand businesses here.

In addition to lowering income tax rates, my proposal will hold harmless Vermonters 65 years and over, and protect middle-income investors by exempting their first $2,500 of long term investment income.

These changes are substantive steps we can take this year to ease the tax pressure on middle-income Vermonters. This is an issue of fundamental fairness and I encourage this Legislature to join me in providing working Vermonters the tax relief they have earned.

Over the last five years, we have made job creation one of our highest priorities. We recognized that growing a strong economy is not the domain of one person, one agency or one group; it is the product of many hands working together, building the infrastructure of success across many disciplines. Our initial efforts have been strong, but we must move forward.

To position Vermont for the next wave of environmentally friendly industry, we must continuously reassess and revitalize our economic development efforts. My comprehensive job creation strategy is the sum of many parts: creating a wireless telecommunications infrastructure, a focus on science and technology in the classroom and targeted incentives for small businesses – all with convergence toward our green economy.

The pace of change is accelerating, and knowledge expanding, at a rate greater than at any other time in human history. The computer and the internet have brought us closer together and given us access to all of the world's information. Keeping up is now a race, and access to the infrastructure of innovation is the difference between success and failure, progress and decline.

Here at home, deep in the Green Mountains, Vermont is ready for this challenge thanks to your willingness to embrace my e-State Initiative. Already, communities throughout Vermont are taking advantage of the changes we made.

In Cabot, residents now have cell service by attaching antennas to a silo – a step that also provides additional income to a working farm. In Bennington County, one company filled an important gap in their coverage by building a Vermont-scale windmill – also on a farm – and attaching their antennas below the turbine. And, thanks to the work of Lt. Governor Dubie, the Northeast Kingdom is the site of a pilot project that will provide a wireless network, with emergency back up by satellite.

These reforms are advancing us steadily toward our goal of a universal network of highspeed wireless phone and internet service that extends to every corner of our state.

To further inspire investments in technology, I'm proposing we invest a quarter-million dollars in two pilot projects – a partnership with Champlain College and the University of Vermont's Center for Emerging Technologies to provide grants to start-up businesses that are developing cutting edge software; and an e-communities grant program to enable more local internet content, discussion forums, wikis and blogs.

There is no doubt that the future of our economy and our environment rests in the hands of technology and our ability to innovate with it – and innovation begins in the classroom.

Over the last several years, the Building Bright Futures initiative has worked to coordinate and support an integrated system of early childhood care, health and education that is fiscally sustainable. Investing in the healthy development of our youngest children and preparing them to arrive at school ready to learn and thrive not only helps students succeed but also reduces special education and human service costs over the long term.

I'm pleased to announce today that the Vermont Community Foundation and the Child Care Fund of Vermont have united with Building Bright Futures and will support this work with a generous investment.

In a speech to our nation's governors, Bill Gates observed, "In math and science, our 4th graders are among the top students in the world. By 8th grade, they're in the middle of the pack. By 12th grade, U.S. students are scoring near the bottom of all industrialized nations." He concluded, "In the international competition to have the biggest and best supply of knowledge workers, America is falling behind."

For Vermont's economy to produce quality, high-paying jobs in the future, we must be competitive with countries around the globe. Our ability to compete depends on our education system.

We must rethink how science, technology, engineering and mathematics are taught in our state. Vermont spends more than nearly any other state on a per capita basis for primary and secondary education; we have the resources to transform our system of education. As taxpayers and parents, we want to know that our children are receiving an education that is preparing them to prosper in the 21st Century.

That is why I have asked the State Board and Department of Education to help schools implement more innovative science, technology, engineering and mathematics curricula.

By rethinking how our education resources are deployed, we can make this transformation. We know that our teachers are ready for the challenge; now let's build a classroom framework to support them.

To ensure that prosperity grows with each generation we must make a continued investment in our human capital. To empower the next generation of workers I propose we invest $8 million – a 14 percent increase over last year's appropriation – in college scholarships and workforce training programs.

Well-trained, educated workers are the lifeblood of Vermont's economy. With strong work ethics and sharp minds, they attract companies that strive to expand and innovate. In fact, Vermonters produce nearly more patents per capita than any other state and – I hate to brag, but – we have been ranked the "Smartest State" two years running by a national research group.

All of this is no surprise. American history has been shaped by the vision and ingenuity of Vermont innovators like John Dewey, Thomas Davenport, Elisha Graves Otis and others whose discoveries improved the quality of life here and abroad. Drawing from the past, scientists are now turning to the 19th century discovery of Davenport – the electric motor, for use in hybrid vehicles – as one solution to the challenge of greenhouse gas emissions.

Now in Vermont, our future is being shaped by innovators producing cutting edge products and ideas that are having the same scope of change in today's economy as Dewey, Davenport and Otis had so many years ago. For example, scientists at Seldon Technologies in Windsor are manipulating carbon nanotube structures to create liquid purification systems that dramatically increase the supply of clean water in the poorest areas of the world.

These types of innovations in science and technology are key to making both our environment cleaner and our economy stronger.

Last year, we kicked off an effort to make Vermont a global center for environmental engineering. This year, I propose we build on that initiative by modifying the Vermont Employment Growth Incentive program to make environmental service companies eligible for significantly larger incentives to create jobs here.

In addition, I ask that the Legislature join me in urging the State retirement boards to designate a percentage of their funds for investment in the creation of green jobs. This could generate up to $10 million in additional capital for investment in entrepreneurship and job creation.

But the single best job creation incentive we can offer small businesses and larger employers alike is to reduce their high tax burden. In all of my travels across Vermont, employers so often – and so unanimously – cite high taxes as a deterrent to more robust growth that I consider the tax reforms I've outlined today as the most basic and important job creation strategy this General Assembly can enact.

Our job creation initiatives must necessarily dovetail with our efforts to keep our environment healthy. I created my Commission on Climate Change to build upon our collective experience as good stewards of the working landscape and lay the foundation for future prosperity.

The Commission's recommendations – and those of its plenary group – are a blueprint for future sustainability and can help us chart our course. The creation of the Vermont Climate Collaborative – a partnership of state, academic, business and other organizations – has united the scientific and technological tools necessary in order to implement these recommendations in an effective, responsible and affordable way.

Vermont is a leader in protecting the environment. Seventy-eight percent of Vermont is working or protected forest and farmland. We lead the nation in energy-efficiency spending, and have the smallest carbon footprint in the nation. In fact, on a yearly basis, we absorb more carbon than we emit.

We have a long history of protecting our natural environment and respecting its cultural and economic value. That is why I am hopeful we will reach a responsible agreement on an all-fuels efficiency program that helps Vermonters make their homes more fuel efficient, lowers their heating costs and reduces greenhouse gas emissions.

Vermont is on the front line of new ideas, new technology and a new way of thinking about our land and its value, but there are some who have held this view for generations. Our farmers, foresters, hunters, anglers and trappers live close to the earth and have much to gain or lose from the work we do.

The tens of thousands of acres of working forests and farms is our "green bank" – a system where investments in good agricultural and forestry practices today will pay dividends to both our environment and economy in the future.

Farmers are continuing to adapt to a changing economy and, through close partnerships all across Vermont, we are seeing good ideas flourish.

Keeping our forests healthy and thriving is also an important tool in our fight against climate change. I have asked the Agency of Natural Resources to work with our forestry community to make available more state land for harvesting.

Through good management practices and partnerships with the sportsmen community, we are taking important steps to protect our wildlife from the diseases that have plagued other states. We are fighting invasive species like sea lamprey with regular and thorough lampricide treatments and we now have the healthiest deer and moose herds in decades.

We must continue to support these important traditional economic sectors through good land and wildlife management practices and a continued investment in the green bank so that the dividends are paid forward to generations ahead who will carry on the traditions of the Green Mountains.

We are a rural state – that means longer drives from home to work and places in between. As a result, vehicles account for nearly half of all carbon emissions in Vermont. The miles traveled aren't the problem; the way we traverse them is.

As gas prices climb, many are taking a second look at fuel efficient cars and trucks and alternatives to single occupancy trips. That's why I propose Go Vermont, a three-pronged approach that provides cost-effective transportation alternatives, promotes the development and availability of cleaner burning biofuels and pushes for increased vehicle emissions standards.

To help Vermonters find smart, affordable commuting alternatives, Go Vermont proposes an online database that will link commuters to carpools, as well as a new system for businesses looking to establish vanpools as a transportation perk for employees. In the last five years, we have increased our investment in public transit by 65% – from nearly $13 million to more than $21 million per year – and we plan to do more still.

Successful vanpool, rideshare and public transit programs require seamless integration between these options and a network of park-and-ride facilities. I propose to double the number of Vermont's park-and-ride spaces over the next decade, and offer more money to communities for the municipal park and ride program.

The State already uses more than 150,000 gallons of biodiesel in its fleet and CCTA buses now run on biodiesel blends. Now, working with the Climate Collaborative, we are preparing for the next step: our lands being managed for new biofuel products – switch grasses, wood, and other vegetation that are renewable, sustainable sources of energy and economic growth. Advanced research is well underway at places like the University of Vermont and the state is poised to become a biofuels leader in New England.

Last week I announced that Vermont would join California in suing the Environmental Protection Agency to allow us – and more than a dozen other states – to impose stricter tailpipe emissions standards. We will not give up the fight on this issue – we will prevail – and we will see significant reductions in our greenhouse gas emissions. While we look for ways to create a more innovative transportation system that will give Vermonters more choices when traveling, we must continue to invest in the Road to Affordability – my approach to transportation funding that puts the preservation of roads, bridges and culverts in balance with other priorities.

Overcoming our challenges and achieving results requires innovation – new thinking, new ideas – and a can-do attitude that inspires government to be more resourceful.

If Vermont is to continue to grow and prosper, we must reexamine the fundamentals of the services we provide and find ways to make improvements. We must bring a new energy to this calling and a pledge to protect those who need us most. And we must reach for the change that will bring a better life to those who still struggle.

Hard-working Vermonters remain at the heart of all we do and for all we strive. They are our strength. The values they carry to work each day are those that will guide us in this session, in our partnership for progress.

As we work to achieve prosperity through affordability, we must now rethink, revitalize and, where necessary, reform the work of government. We are ready for the challenge – this time of change requires it.

God bless each of you and the great State of Vermont.

Fourth Inaugural Address
January 8, 2009

MR. PRESIDENT, MR. Speaker, distinguished guests, my fellow Vermonters:

One hundred seventy three years ago farmers, businessmen, and lawyers from across Vermont met here for the 1836 session of the General Assembly. Among them, a minister and headmaster of the Orleans County Grammar School took his seat as the member from Brownington.

Alexander Twilight was a pioneer. A native of Corinth, Twilight's life was devoted to public service as a preacher, educator and legislator. When he took his oath so many years ago, Twilight made quiet history as the first African-American to serve in a state legislature.

In less than two weeks we will observe the swearing in of our next president, opening a new chapter in America's history. We can all be proud of how far we have come to this momentous occasion – one that Alexander Twilight could barely have imagined when he served in this body over a century and a half ago. Let there be no doubt that our system of government, the institutions of our nation, and the American spirit endure stronger than ever.

Each time I climb the steps to this podium, I am reminded of the many great leaders whose footsteps I trace, and am humbled to share this honor with them. I am deeply grateful for the confidence Vermonters have placed in me and for God's grace that touches us all. I am blessed to have such a wonderful family, many of whom join me here today, including my wife, Dorothy, and my son, Matt.

As I look out across this chamber, I see old friends and new faces, all of us charged by the people to address the great challenges that face our state. I offer my sincere congratulations to new and returning members of our legislature, as well as Lieutenant Governor Dubie and other statewide elected officials. I also want to offer my congratulations to Speaker Smith.

Voters have again returned a legislature controlled by one party balanced by an executive of another and they expect us to work together. Whether you sit as a Democrat, Republican, Progressive or Independent, we are all Vermonters first; and to a person we have been entrusted with a monumental task – to steer our state through rocky shoals.

Together, we shall not fail.

We gather today for the time-honored rite of inauguration, an important symbol of our vibrant democracy. An inauguration marks a gateway between past and future, an occasion of starting anew. Indeed, a time of transition is where we find our state.

On factory floors, in small businesses and around kitchen tables, and even in this very hall, we share the anxiety of a nation on edge. As moms and dads, friends and neighbors, we feel the painful effects of recession sweeping across our country and around the world.

Vermont has been pulled into this national downturn, the depth and breadth of which we have not seen for generations. The foundation of our economic security has been fractured. We have seen pyramids built on greed crumble and institutions thought indestructible disappear.

For too long, too many have held the mistaken belief that we could live beyond our means – that we could buy now and pay later – convinced that easy credit would allow us to have what we could not afford. Many thought revenues would always rise and difficult decisions could be deferred.

That misguided notion has brought us to this time of great collapse. If we ignore the modern parables of Wall Street and Washington, we risk their fate – and a future that spurns our Yankee forbearers who carved this state from the granite of "temperance, industry and frugality."

Today, I present a plan for Vermont to direct its own future, free from the ties that bind us to the status quo. Rather than follow blindly, we will lead boldly.

The discussion about how to balance a lean state budget will consume the greater part of this biennium – and appropriately so.

Consider the realities we are facing: we have already trimmed $43 million from our current year budget and, in the coming weeks, the legislature will consider an additional $46 million in rescissions. When the state's economists meet next week, we could again see revenues decline; further requiring cuts to balance our budget. And our challenges don't stop there; in fiscal 2010 we expect to have a shortfall of more than $150 million.

In the past, we have looked to four primary fixes to mend holes in our state balance sheet – spending down reserves, relying on federal aid, raising taxes, and deep spending cuts – but none of them, whether alone or taken together, are adequate to address the current economic crisis.

The most oft-cited approach is to use the state's stabilization reserves – that is, the "rainy day funds" – as a quick patch to the problem. There is no doubt it's raining, but no one knows just how long this storm will last. To use the rainy day funds now is to ignore the severity of this recession in hopes the danger passes. Once we use our reserves, they are gone and it will likely take us years to replenish them. There is a right time to use the rainy day funds – when we experience an unanticipated drop in state revenues – but now, when other choices remain, is not that time.

Following the recession of 1991 the state had no reserve funds and few alternatives but to cut programs deeply and raise taxes sharply. Eighteen years later, the economic conditions we face rival that downturn – but that's where the similarities end. State government is much better suited to weather this storm with full reserves, years of balanced budgets, and the highest bond rating in New England – all variables absent from the 1991 equation.

Further, working Vermonters are exposed to the risk of volatile markets, more so than in previous downturns. Families have watched college savings dwindle and their modest investments falter. Folks who have worked their whole lives have seen retirement accounts lose half their value. The personal reserves of average Vermonters have suffered, leaving smaller and smaller nest eggs.

In addition to that, Vermonters have no capacity for higher taxes – another approach advanced to shore up state coffers. In previous recessions, the state has raised taxes calling the increases "temporary" or under the guise of a "tax shift." But when our fortunes improved, some taxes remained and the revenues were spent. Economists across the political spectrum agree that to raise taxes now would only slow a recovery, especially in Vermont, where our total tax burden is among the very highest in the nation.

I have heard recent proposals that would raise the top marginal tax rate by 37%, placing Vermont at the top of the tax heap – 26% above the next highest state – a dubious distinction especially as we compete with our neighbors for jobs and industry. Our earned income tax rates would be 90% greater than New York, 145% greater than Massachusetts, and infinitely greater than New Hampshire, which has no such tax. How many employers – especially in difficult times – would willingly choose to curb returns in order to pay more taxes?

It is unfair and unacceptable for us to expect the people of Vermont – who are making difficult budget choices everyday in their homes and businesses – to pay for an unwillingness to make tough budget decisions.

While I look forward to working with President-elect Obama and his new administration in coming the years – waiting on Washington to pass an economic recovery package is not a responsible stand-alone option. Although we are preparing for an influx of federal money, we must remember that any help is only temporary. If we do not get our fiscal house in order today, we will find ourselves on a cliff's edge when the money runs out – forced to make more drastic decisions tomorrow.

Given the magnitude of the growing budget gap, it would be shortsighted to only cut our way out of this problem. While economic contraction demands belt-tightening and we cannot avoid rescissions in nearly every area of government, this approach alone will not position us to emerge from this downturn ready to grow. If we nickel and dime services to keep the budget in balance, we will quickly reach a point where our programs are no longer able to serve their purposes.

Now is not the time to rest on old notions. Now is not the time to spare sacred cows. Now is the time we must summon the courage to forge lasting solutions and reject the patchworks of the past.

From great collapse, we must rise again with a new framework for progress – one that sets government on a sustainable path through the transformation of education, human services and economic development. Only by doing so can we rebuild our economy, create good paying jobs and protect the most vulnerable during these difficult times.

As Vermonters, our cause for optimism remains great – it is rooted in our shared history, our commitment to one another, and the promise of a better tomorrow. It is found in an old farmer and a young family; in our lessons passed down from parent to child; in the hunters, anglers and trappers who give new life to old traditions; and in entrepreneurs creating new opportunities for our people.

It is manifest in the pride we share for those who protect our communities – our police, firefighters and EMTs – and in the brave men and women of our armed forces who risk their lives far from the Green Mountains to preserve our most cherished values. I want to take a moment to recognize representatives of our National Guard who join us in the balcony today.

Our work in recent years has prepared us to meet today's challenges. During our nation's last recession in 2003, we passed the largest jobs package in state history. As we emerged from that downturn we streamlined government, and expanded access to health care. We strengthened our commitment to the next generation, increased bonding capacity and made new investments in our roads, bridges and culverts, and provided incentives for green businesses to succeed – while balancing the budget each year.

To keep Vermont competitive in a rapidly changing world economy we worked together to create the Vermont Telecommunications Authority – setting a course to achieve our goal of becoming the first true "e-state," where everyone has access to the tools of the 21st century.

Last year we took immediate steps to spur economic activity and temper the effects of the looming downturn. The Economic Growth Initiative – which included a successful sales tax holiday to help working families and boost Vermont retailers – was a needed bridge in a time of turmoil. And the Fuel and Food Partnership is coordinating services among the state, private agencies and local communities to ensure that vulnerable Vermonters have the resources they need during this already harsh winter.

But to preserve these valuable gains, the time has come for our state to embrace this new framework – where the real needs of people intersect with the true capacity of government to serve.

Ingrained in some areas of government is an institutional momentum that demands more resources regardless of taxpayers' ability to support their growth. The recent downgrades in our revenue forecasts and the bleak outlook for the coming fiscal year have shone a bright light on the imbalance we now find among different functions of government.

The best examples can be found in two areas – general education and Medicaid. Combined, in state dollars alone, they account for sixty-three cents of every tax dollar spent in Vermont. These areas of government continue to grow year after year without the same checks and constraints as other important services.

We must advance beyond these obsolete models and move to a modern approach – breaking down longstanding walls to achieve equilibrium among many important priorities and support lasting economic security.

As the parents of two boys who attended public school in Vermont, Dorothy and I know the value of a quality education. As the grandson, son and son-in-law, brother and brother-in-law, nephew and uncle of educators, I recognize the great inspiration teachers bring to the classroom every day.

Vermonters are rightly proud of the quality of our public education system and the tremendous caliber of our teachers. Pride, however, does not excuse us from the necessary and important changes to make education spending sustainable for the long term.

As we examine the current fiscal challenges, it is clear that our public education system is on a collision course with economic reality – threatening not only the dwindling capacity of taxpayers, but also our responsibility to fund essential services for vulnerable Vermonters.

In the last five years, Vermont has experienced an education spending expansion funded by property tax increases and general funds. Assuming the fiscal 2010 current law projections, spending from the education fund will have increased by nearly $283 million since fiscal 2006, or a 23% increase. Over the same period, statewide school enrollment has dropped over 4,300 students, or a 4.4% decrease. This means that since 2006, for every student who left the rolls, schools added – not reduced – $65,000 in costs.

While unfunded federal mandates and inflationary increases drive a portion of these costs, the biggest portion is attributed to increases in staff count. Since 1997, student enrollment has fallen by almost 10,000 children, or 10%, but school staffs have increased by 3,500 positions, or 22%. Put another way, for every three students who left the rolls, schools have added one staff position.

In contrast, we are looking at the jobless rate rising every month, with thousands of Vermonters added to the unemployment rolls since last summer. State government is trimming its workforce, some businesses are reducing hours, and others are closing their doors completely. Everyone is facing cutbacks during this difficult time. But still, education spending for 2010 is expected to grow 6.1% per pupil. Recent newspaper articles report proposed school budget increases of 5%, 8%, and even 11%. Property tax bills are expected to grow an average of 6%, even after income sensitivity payments.

Expansion like this is unsustainable in any season, and especially when our economy is facing such severe retrenchment.

Our current education funding system is failing taxpayers and local voters. For over a decade, Vermonters, in every corner of the state, have borne the heavy burden of rising property taxes under Act 60. It is wrong for one third of all tax dollars to be spent on a system only a handful can explain. When enrollments decline but property tax bills increase – and when communities are forced to vote budgets without knowing the real consequence of those decisions, it is clear that our system does not work.

Act 60 and Act 68 are fundamentally broken and beyond repair. Piecemeal changes cannot mend a system that is so far out of balance. Only a wholesale transformation will return control to communities and put education funding on a sustainable course for the future.

There is no one size fits all approach to education. Each school district must determine what works best for its students. But maintaining the status quo is not in our kids' best interests. Building an education system for the future requires a willingness to recognize the realities of declining enrollments across the state.

Now is the time to build a new system – one that is fair and equitable, and respects the voice of voters, the pocketbooks of taxpayers and the potential of our students. Too often, politics has stood in the way of change. That is why, with a sincere commitment to progress, I ask the Legislature to work with me to establish a collaborative process for fresh ideas – bringing together thoughtful individuals with broad range of perspectives to design an education funding system that is simple, transparent and sustainable. We must also be prepared to examine school consolidation, governance, special education costs, and other opportunities to achieve efficiencies.

I will seek your suggestions on the best minds for this high priority. I understand the magnitude of this proposal, but with so much at stake and inaction threatening the economic security of countless Vermonters, we must work together to take this important step.

While launching this process is essential to rebuilding our education finance system, property taxpayers cannot wait another year for relief. In order to create a funding bridge until a new system is established, I propose a common-sense measure to freeze per-pupil spending for schools and categorical grants at current levels. When we consider what government, businesses and families are facing, level funding is a fair approach.

Further, we will strengthen local control by holding school districts directly responsible for tax increases. During this bridge year, if a school wants to raise additional money above level-funding, it can ask voters to fund the increase entirely through its residential tax rate, up to a level that respects the Brigham decision.

I also propose we end property tax subsidies for Vermonters making over $75,000 in order to lower tax rates even further for all payers.

By taking these steps, we'll be able to effectively reduce property tax rates by 4 cents for a total of $44 million. The statewide rates can each be cut by at least 2 cents, that is $24 million. Further, the spending freeze results in additional residential property tax reductions of another $20 million as projected increases in per pupil spending are avoided. In fact, the state will collect no more from residential taxpayers next year than it has this year – a welcome change for struggling Vermonters.

All across our state dedicated volunteer school boards are working diligently to craft budgets in time for Town Meeting. I know they are facing difficult decisions – state government is struggling with the same real time adjustments. And I acknowledge that my plan represents a departure from usual practice – but we are in unusual times. That is why I am committed to working closely with school districts to give them the flexibility they need to consider budgets that are level-funded.

Property taxes are not the only source of revenue for education spending. The general fund of state government provides a substantial share of school funding.

Without changes to the current system, the state is expected to transfer $298 million from the general fund – nearly a quarter of available resources – to the education fund in fiscal 2010. This transfer, which will have increased over $38 million since 2006, has been held completely harmless during the recent rounds of rescissions.

Further, the State Teachers' Retirement System is directly supported with general fund money and has not been subject to reductions during recent cut-backs. In fiscal 2010, the general fund is expected to contribute at least $40 million as the employer's share of contribution to support the system. This approach is a vestige of the past and effectively allows schools to set salaries detached from the true cost of the benefits.

In other words, the education fund has not shared any of the sacrifice seen by other areas of state government. If we continue to excuse education spending from equal treatment, we force health care and human services – the lion's share of the remaining general fund – to shoulder the burden of balancing a responsible budget. That is not a realistic, or compassionate, option.

To put these disparities between the general and education funds in context, we should step back and look at the big picture. According to current estimates for the next fiscal year, we need to reduce benefits and cut programs – primarily in human services – by at least $150 million out of a general fund budget of less than $1.2 billion. Meanwhile, funding for K-12 education is expected to increase $63 million in the $1.4 billion education fund.

In fact, with current projections, while the education fund will have grown 23% since 2006, the general fund will have actually decreased 2% – meaning that we will be spending less in state government in our fiscal 2010 budget than we did in fiscal 2006.

If we do not take action to restore the equilibrium between the general and education funds, we risk devastating spending cuts. I propose placing the obligation for funding the teachers' retirement system where it belongs – in the education fund. This $40 million would leverage $97 million in state and federal

Global Commitment money and reduce the need to cut critical programs for vulnerable Vermonters. I also propose linking the general fund transfer to the education fund to changes in the level of general government spending. This is a reasonable approach that respects the capacity of taxpayers.

Further, a close examination of spending for public education reveals a startling imbalance among our funding levels for early education, K-12, and higher education. We spend relatively little on early education – are among the highest in the nation for primary and secondary education – and near the bottom for higher education. We must begin to reshape this skewed distribution of resources.

Access to affordable, quality early care and education provides a dual benefit: it lays the building blocks for a successful future, ensuring children arrive at kindergarten ready to learn; and, it removes the single biggest barrier for parents in poverty to move into the workforce. At the other end of the spectrum, Vermont's colleges and state university are among the most expensive in the nation and for too many Vermonters, simply out of reach.

To move our system of education into the 21st Century we must strengthen our commitment to creating a continuum of learning that begins in early childhood and never ends, providing the necessary opportunities to Vermonters throughout their lives.

A real investment in lifelong learning is an investment in an individual's economic independence. Indeed, few things are more important to establishing a strong and growing economy than the education and training of our workforce. That's why, despite budget challenges, I propose a 20% increase in early and higher education as a first step to address spending disparities and prepare Vermonters, young and old, for future success.

I realize that there are some who have an interest in maintaining the current system. They will challenge any data and idea that calls into question the need to move our system of education out of the past and into the future. But we were not elected to safeguard the needs of one interest over another – we were elected to do our best for all Vermonters. I ask this assembly to join me in revitalizing our education system to better serve our children and make needed investments in the future of Vermont.

But the transformation we need requires a shift not only in thinking and spending, but in structure as well. The final step is to seek the benefits from an integration of the University of Vermont and the Vermont State Colleges into a single organization. We have real gems in our state university and colleges, and with a commitment to progress, we can establish a higher education system better positioned to meet the needs of the student bodies. This marriage of resources – from infrastructure to administration, programs to athletics – will allow each college the freedom and flexibility to better focus on targeted academics offering the very best to each student.

I will charge a working task force with the responsibility to find academic and administrative efficiencies that will be achieved through consolidation of our university and state college systems. I will ask the task force to report with recommendations by November 15th.

Underpinning everything we will do in the coming session is our obligation to the most at risk in our society. We must make certain that those with the greatest need – children and vulnerable elders, working poor Vermonters, those with developmental disabilities and mental health challenges, and the indigent – are protected. But in order for government to ensure that the programs and benefits are secure, we must chart a course that is financially sustainable and outcome-based.

The prospect of belt-tightening in state government understandably draws concerns from community providers, advocates and consumers of state benefits. I share the concerns about the impact of budget decisions on individuals and the programs and services they need.

Make no mistake: these are tough conversations, made tougher with real heartache and real adversity. After all, in a state like Vermont, these stories are not statistics – but rather the family, friends and neighbors entwined in our daily lives. But while these conversations are difficult, they are the right conversations to have at a time like this.

The first element of protecting the most vulnerable is to ensure the near-term solvency of benefit programs, while working to create sustainability in the long-term. Our first of its kind Global Commitment to Health waiver was a major milestone in addressing our challenges in the Medicaid budget. But even with Global Commitment, caseload increases outpace resources with a bigger and bigger portion of the state budget needed to fill the gap.

Although our federal partner in Medicaid is expected to help with increased funds through the economic recovery package, that alone will not ameliorate increasing pressures on the human service budget. We must take immediate steps to set this vital network of programs on a sustainable path.

Right now 25% of Vermonters receive some form of Medicaid assistance, among the highest percentages in the nation. There are principally two ways to make Medicaid sustainable: either we can exclude populations above a certain income level and eliminate their services, or we can realign benefits and share costs to fit responsible budgets. To me, the option of eliminating health care coverage for many Vermonters in order to preserve a generous benefit for a few is unjust in such a challenging time. The philosophy of sharing the sacrifice broadly must be part of any proposal we advance.

We must also guarantee that each dollar is spent with a focus on quality of life and the goal of future independence.

Our efforts to provide a healthy lifestyle discount in the private health insurance market should be mirrored in our Medicaid program. Encouraging Vermonters to make better choices when it comes to their health and well-being is a critical component of our innovative health care reforms, and the Vermont Blueprint for Health is the cornerstone of these efforts. We should align Medicaid with these goals and work to reward beneficiaries who eat nutritiously, stay in shape and live a clean life, free from drugs and smoking. By offering lower premiums for healthy choices, we can provide a tangible incentive to empower Medicaid recipients to take responsibility for their own well-being and, at the same time, lower health care costs.

While the vast majority of beneficiaries and providers in our human services network are honest, we have all heard stories about some who exploit the system. Such unscrupulous acts threaten to shortchange those most in need. I have asked the Agency of Human Services to review the state's response to those who falsify information to obtain government benefits or payments, including consumers who abuse prescription drug benefits. At a time when we are forced to consider significant cuts to programs, we must look for ways to guarantee that the programs we have are serving only those Vermonters for whom they were intended.

It is reasonable for the state to ask beneficiaries to assist us in enhancing their individual health and welfare. We must focus our assistance, invest in Vermonters, and ensure we are building transformational bridges: from poverty to economic success; from chronic illness to health; from drug dependence to independence. That's the covenant: the state provides assistance and beneficiaries work to amplify the state's investment and improve their lives.

Although common-sense changes to our human service programs are vital, there is no substitute for a good-paying job to bring real renewal into an individual's life. While it's hard to think about creating jobs as businesses close and lay off employees, now is the time for us to redouble our efforts to support existing companies, encourage entrepreneurship and attract new employers by transforming our economy to meet the demands of the 21st century.

During the fall I introduced a series of proposals – an Economic Growth Plan – to make our state more competitive and position Vermont to be on the first wave of recovery. As the economy continues to soften, it is important that we act to enhance our economic development efforts and pass this practical plan in the first 100 days of the session.

Many of the principles that bind these proposals together are shared across the political spectrum. We understand the value of renewable, clean and affordable energy. We've seen the power of information and the potential of technology. And we know that in a rapidly changing economy, our ability to grow and attract innovative, emerging industries will be the difference between success and failure.

That is why I have called for the development of Green Growth Zones to join commercial, residential and renewable energy facilities together in an arrangement that benefits an energy producer with access to a ready market, and benefits businesses and individuals with reduced rates for clean power. And that is why it makes sense to provide greater regulatory certainty to assist in the creation of a Smart Grid for Vermont.

As part of last year's Economic Growth Initiative, we provided a higher level VEGI incentive to green industries. By expanding this successful program to technology-based employers, such as software developers, we can encourage growth in this fast moving sector of our economy.

Whether it is a more fuel-efficient car or a breakthrough in biomedicine, Vermont must aspire to be the home of innovation and invention. By enticing entrepreneurs through the Vermont Innovation Challenge, we can help meet the needs and employment potential of our workforce.

As I travel Vermont and talk with employers, too often I hear the same stories about the time, expense and uncertainty of obtaining necessary permits and approvals to begin a project to grow their companies.

I believe that some in Vermont have lost sight of what a permit application really means.

It is easy to characterize applications in the negative: this project will add that much traffic or require this much mitigation.

But to me, a permit application really says something very positive.

It says, "I'm hiring."

It says, "I'm prepared to make an investment in Vermont."

It says, "I'm ready to put down roots in this community and create jobs."

For many Vermonters what that permit application really means – above all else – is the difference between checking in for work and waiting for an unemployment check.

When an employer has made the commitment to grow responsibly in Vermont, we must make the commitment to speed the process from permit application to shovels in the ground.

Over the years, we have advanced reforms to parts and pieces of the process, sometimes with success – as we had five years ago in streamlining appeals – but most often without closure. The current system remains a labyrinth, fraught with unpredictability, which threatens job creation for years ahead – unless we are prepared to make substantive changes that will modernize the system.

As we strive to protect that which is so special about Vermont, we must recognize that a "working landscape" requires Vermonters to be actually working - not simply admiring the view.

We must preserve and strengthen our gold standard of environmental protection, but we can do so while making it easier for companies to invest in

Vermont and grow with certainty. We can build a better, more practical system based on clear guidelines, professional assistance, a good dose of trust and strong penalties for non-compliance.

I propose we broaden Act 250 so proposals are not only judged on impacts, but also on the positive economic, social, or cultural benefits that may flow from a project into a community or region.

We must bring greater predictability to all interested parties by ensuring that once you've obtained your permit from an agency of state government, that permit will not be challenged in an Act 250 proceeding.

Further, we must expedite the chilling and costly effect of our lengthy appeals process by instituting "on the record review" – one formal hearing, where all evidence is submitted and examined.

Finally, we must expand the use of the self-certifications, general permits and permits by rule that are now used in stormwater, air pollution control and other programs. Instead of complex front-end regulation, we can provide clear guidance to businesses and trust them to design appropriate systems with the help of a recognized professional, obtain a general permit, and move towards better and faster construction.

Businesses will not be let off the hook from environmental protection. Non-compliance will bring costly penalties, motivating developers to complete legally and environmentally sound projects. Furthermore, self-certification will allow agency staff to spend more time in the field ensuring compliance, rather than micro managing proposed permits upfront.

I have directed the Secretary of Natural Resources to examine every permitting program within the Agency, identify those for which self-certification and other strategies make sense, and design approaches for each.

By creating a more responsive regulatory process we will uphold our cherished environmental standards and at the same time allow our state to grow and thrive.

In the short term, however, the extraordinary realities of the current economic crisis demand immediate action. I have asked my administration to work with the legislature and others to create the Vermont Economic Response Team, which will marshal all available public and private resources to assist companies at risk. Similar to the Fuel and Food Partnership model, the Response Team will cut through red tape, expedite the deployment of resources and examine temporary measures to help a business that is in trouble. When Vermont companies are in distress, I want to be absolutely sure that we do everything possible to help them weather this storm.

Agriculture and forest products remain pillars of our rural communities and, like other industries, are struggling.

Unfortunately, we expect the price of milk to drop significantly this spring. Although there is little the state can do to insulate dairy farmers from the volatile national milk pricing system, especially during these lean fiscal times, the Agency of Agriculture has been working closely with counterparts in New York and Pennsylvania, and the northeast dairy cooperatives to offset falling milk prices.

We will continue to work diligently with our congressional delegation to explore all options to help our traditional industries survive a difficult economic climate in the coming year.

While education, social services and jobs are all vital to the future of Vermont, the safety of our children trumps all else. The tragic events of the last year are a sobering reminder that more must always be done to keep violent sexual predators off our streets and away from our children.

I am confident that we can work together to quickly pass a comprehensive package of laws that focus on prevention, strengthens investigations and prosecutions, requires stiffer sentencing – particularly a 25-year mandatory minimum sentence – and enhanced supervision for sexual offenders. We have no time to waste in ensuring that law enforcement, the courts, families and communities have the tools they need to keep the children of Vermont safe.

I would like to take a moment to address the more than 8,000 Vermonters who work in state government and make this $4.3 billion enterprise run. State government remains the most far-reaching organization in the state. And now more than ever, our fellow

Vermonters need us to lead by example – to find in every department, in every division, new ways to generate economic activity and ensure that those who most depend on our services receive them. I know you don't always receive the credit you deserve, but your work has a tangible impact on the lives of those you serve. And I am confident that at day's end the work we do will help our state emerge quickly and strongly from this downturn.

For the moment the clouds of recession have obscured our view of a more prosperous future. The task ahead is difficult and demanding, but Vermont will succeed. We will achieve our goals and realize the full potential of a people whose legacy is the diligence of its industry and the inspiration of its innovation.

Today, as our will commands, Vermont moves forward.

We will move together, past old ideas and embrace new solutions. We will address our challenges directly and completely. We will re-balance and strengthen our system of education, secure our social safety net and, most importantly, we will create a new, lasting framework for sustained growth.

Today, we inaugurate new ideas and real solutions to restore our economic security, awaken our optimism and produce new opportunities.

When this work is complete, and when the clouds of recession lift, we will look back at this session of the General Assembly as the moment we ushered in a new era of prosperity in our state's history.

God bless each you and the great state of Vermont.

2010 State of the State
January 7, 2010

MR. PRESIDENT, MR. Speaker, members of the General Assembly, distinguished guests, my fellow Vermonters:

Before I begin today, I want to acknowledge the loss of two dedicated public servants, Representative Ira Trombley and Representative Rick Hube. Our thoughts are with their families and we are grateful for their contributions to our state.

Each morning the people of our state awake with a simple hope: to build a better future for themselves, their families and the generations that will follow. Throughout our history, Vermonters have mustered the strength to meet each day with the wisdom, ingenuity, and tireless work ethic of our Yankee forebearers.

From towns, villages and cities, they've elected representatives to bring that same focus to the People's House. It is here where we carry forth our proud tradition of self-government – always striving to forge a state, nation and world better than before.

Today, that work is far from done. In these uncertain times, we must transform our public and economic framework by redesigning how we deliver state services and refocusing efforts to create jobs and ensure economic security for Vermonters. Out of necessity and because it is the right thing to do, we must act now to write the next chapter in the proud history of Vermont.

As we gather to embark on this work, let us keep in mind our friends and neighbors serving in Iraq and Afghanistan, and those preparing to leave. Our service men and women are asked to defend self-government and individual freedom in a part of the world where there is too little of both. Their efforts contribute to a noble legacy forged by Vermonters from the Battle of Bennington to Cedar Creek, from the beaches of Normandy to the streets of Baghdad. These brave men and women embody the best of the Vermont spirit and their sacrifice inspires us all.

I've seen, time and again, the will of Vermonters to change, reform and make better this great state. I've seen what can be accomplished when we work together, putting the public good before self interest. Indeed, the last decade has been full of such accomplishments.

When it comes to keeping our neighborhoods safe, there will always be more to do, but our shared commitment gives me confidence that we will be ever vigilant. I'm proud that we have worked together to send a clear message to sexual predators that they will be prosecuted and severely punished in Vermont. And while illicit drugs still destroy too many young lives, the DETER program has increased our efforts with better education, prevention, treatment and rehabilitation for those who suffer from addiction, as well as strengthened enforcement against drug dealers.

Vermont's commitment to our natural resources is unwavering. The Clean and Clear Action Plan is a model for how government, citizen groups, farmers and others can work together to reduce pollution in our waterways. We've led on climate change by partnering with other northeastern states in the Regional Greenhouse Gas Initiative. And we were the first state to join California in adopting more stringent standards for automobile emissions, ultimately forcing the federal government to follow our lead. Our environmental leadership is a source of pride that sets us apart and gives us a leg-up in the green economy.

That Vermont is the healthiest state comes as no surprise. It's in our nature to be active, enjoy our outdoors, and eat healthy. We've taken our message to young Vermonters with our Fit and Healthy Kids program, to working Vermonters with our Worksite Wellness programs and to older Vermonters with my Commission on Healthy Aging. And we've achieved groundbreaking health reforms with our innovative Blueprint for Health, the Global Commitment waiver and Catamount Health. In just two years, we have seen our uninsured rate drop by 25 percent. And with the Blueprint, we're beginning to bend the curve on costs. By combining coordinated care, health information technology and payment system reform, we are eliminating duplicative, unnecessary services and creating a more efficient and effective health care system.

These common sense approaches are not only being emulated in Washington; they are delivering real results here at home. Rhonda Rose of St. Johnsbury is a Blueprint for Health success story. Rhonda's chronic illness was a significant challenge, draining her bank account, as well as drawing heavily on state resources. Her local community health team stepped in and made a full assessment, taking the necessary actions to get her health back on track and prevent expensive emergency room visits. Not only has Rhonda's health improved, but she's been able to go back to work and is enjoying life again. I'm very pleased that Rhonda can join us in the balcony today.

As we look to make programs and services better and more affordable, we need only to look to these achievements, particularly in health care, as a beacon for the kind of positive change that's possible when we work together toward a common goal. In that spirit we must partner again.

Our successes are threatened by massive budget shortfalls, unfunded liabilities and a broken system of education funding. Working families have been battered by recession and employers weakened by state policies that are barriers to job creation.

The trajectory of the Vermont economy for the next decade will be shaped by our decisions this year. If we are content to limp out of this recession, hobbled by flat job growth, we can choose to recycle old ideas and hope for a different outcome. But if we want to spring out of this recession – strong and nimble – we must have the heart to reform, the wisdom to act and the courage to stand against those who will say it cannot be done.

Mere "recovery" is not enough for Vermonters who have persevered through this long season of decline. We must strive for a healthy and growing economy, prepared to compete with states next door and countries around the world. Prepared to compete – and win. These times demand new thinking – they demand bold action – and they demand it now.

A balanced and responsible budget is at the core of getting our state on track. Make no mistake: there will be many unenviable choices among worthy priorities. The solutions required to close the gap will invariably draw objection and complaint. Although we will consider constructive alternatives, this is not the time nor the place for the reflexive defense of the status quo.

If we put off hard decisions for yet another year, we will be left with a cumulative deficit of a half billion dollars over the next three years – our worst choice, by far.

Two days ago, we took an important step in the right direction when I was joined by legislative leaders to announce the results of our collaborative effort to find sustainable savings.

Representatives Obuchowski and Sweaney, Senator Snelling and my Administration worked together on a plan that will save $38 million in the General Fund next year – resulting in millions more in savings down the road. This is the type of break from business-as-usual that is essential for our success. By setting this agreement in law by the end of this month, we can move forward with greater certainty on the tougher budget challenges ahead.

Access to our courts and the timely resolution of cases is one of the fundamental obligations of state government. Ensuring that Vermont's judicial system is financially sustainable is of utmost importance. In the past year, the Judiciary has pitched in to help meet our fiscal challenges. While furloughs and occasional Court closings were necessary, they are not acceptable long-term solutions.

The recommendations of the Commission on Judicial Operations provide a blueprint for a stronger and more affordable system of justice. I know some ideas are controversial; some changes depart from long-held traditions; and the necessary rebalancing will affect certain districts and constituencies. But like all of our decisions this year, narrow interests must take a backseat to the broader public interest. The General Assembly must give these recommendations due consideration, finding in them, as I have, a path forward.

These are just two steps in the process of building a balanced, responsible and sustainable budget. The spending plan I will present on January 19th will be informed by these and other efforts underway to address our $150 million General Fund shortfall.

With 40 percent of the total state budget spent in human services, many of the tough choices we must make will affect this system. Service providers will be asked to find efficiencies. Some beneficiaries will have to accept reductions in order to preserve benefits for the most vulnerable.

Still some programs and grants will be significantly reduced or eliminated. But we will lessen these impacts by redesigning how we deliver services. To assure that Vermont's safety net is sound even in the most challenging economic times, we must reform.

Our redesigned system will be easy to navigate, with a single point of entry and flexible options, catering to individual needs. We will work with service providers to ease their administrative burden. Our focus will be on outcomes for Vermonters – providing a clear and direct path back to health, employment and independence. Success will be measured not by how much we give, but by how well we help Vermonters move from assistance to self-sufficiency.

While our budget deficits are daunting, we must always keep in mind that they are a symptom – not the cause – of the everyday challenges of the people of our state. Last year, Vermonters median household income fell by nearly $1,900 from the year before. Our workforce shed more than 10,000 jobs since October 2008. And Vermont's population is among the slowest growing in the nation, with more people leaving the Green Mountain State than moving in.

These numbers tell a sobering story. If we want to keep the jobs we have, if we want to get our small businesses to succeed in a global economy, if we want to attract rather than turn away people and potential companies, then we need to focus on the fundamentals.

Employers of all sizes, in all sectors, have made clear what they need to re-start the engine of our prosperity: lower taxes; universal broadband and wireless; reliable, affordable energy; a well-trained workforce; and an education system that is top-notch without being top-dollar.

A Vermonter who is employed doesn't need an unemployment check; a Vermonter earning a good wage doesn't need state assistance to help pay the bills; and a young Vermonter with a stable job can put down roots and strengthen a community. That's why I call on lawmakers to join me in putting the economic success of Vermonters first.

The single most consequential action we can take to encourage a healthy economy is to address the crushing weight of Vermont's tax burden. Time and again, employers tell me that our heavy taxation is stifling job creation, making it more difficult to retain our next generation. Increasing taxes, yet again, would only hasten our disturbing demographic and employment trends.

To spur job growth, we need to take steps to roll back last year's key tax increases, encourage growing companies with proven incentives and shore up the unemployment insurance trust fund with a responsible, balanced approach.

As you might remember, I opposed the income and estate tax increases passed by this Assembly last year. Those changes have swelled the ranks of Vermonters who are looking at other states – like New Hampshire or Florida – for their new, permanent residences.

For those who are quick to say "good riddance," think again. When we lose a long-time Vermonter to another state, we lose the community involvement, we lose the charitable giving, and we lose those deep roots that give Vermont its unique character – not to mention the tax revenue.

While my first choice would be to unwind all of the increases at once, that is not feasible in the face of our current condition. Instead, we must address the critical components most detrimental to job creation as soon as possible and commit to buy back all of the increases – plus make additional tax cuts when the economy improves.

Governor Dick Snelling's plan to respond to the recession of the early 1990's was invoked many times last year to justify tax increases. But one key element of that plan – one that made it palatable at the time – was omitted. I ask the Legislature to, this year, honor the second critical part of the Snelling plan and enact a sunset for its tax hikes, while continuing to lock down the income tax rates. This action will send a clear signal to Vermonters and businesses that we are listening to their concerns and working to meet their needs.

Further, the estate tax was increased last year to collect a greater portion of assets from deceased Vermonters. This change is particularly unfair to farmers whose assets are not easily mobile. It is a punitive tax that discourages farmers and small business owners from passing along their life's work to sons and daughters. And, in the long run, it will have a tangible, detrimental effect on our revenues, as individuals change their residency to another state. I ask legislators to join me in rolling back this tax increase.

Until we lower our overall tax rates to competitive levels, we need programs like the Vermont Employment Growth Incentive as part of our economic development tool kit. Since 2007, this employment program has authorized incentives for nearly 2,000 new jobs, and saved more than 2,000 existing jobs that might have been lost if employers chose to relocate out of state. The program has helped employers of all shapes and sizes, from small firms such as Vermont

Timber Frames of Bennington, to medium-sized employers like SB Electronics in Barre, to large companies like Green Mountain Coffee Roasters. As long as our tax burden remains high, I propose eliminating the VEGI cap to keep pace with the growing demand from potential employers.

These tax proposals are a critical step in our efforts to restore employer confidence and send a message that Vermont is ready to compete for jobs. Unfortunately, the cumulative effect of these changes will still not equal the inevitable increase in unemployment taxes. That is why we must act this year to make our unemployment insurance trust fund solvent. A modest reduction in benefits coupled with phased-in increases in the taxable wage base is the prudent course to getting this fund back on solid footing.

There are additional investments in economic development that we can make now. I renew my call to use nearly $9 million from the federal stimulus act for job creation. This money will help train workers, provide access to capital for small businesses and farms, promote tourism and enhance our telecommunications infrastructure. Employers have told us what they need – now is the time for us to listen and act.

When a company comes to our state with 50, 30 or even 15 new jobs, we trip over ourselves to welcome them. When a valued employer is looking to expand or move elsewhere, we work feverishly to keep them here. We have such a company: one that employs hundreds of Vermonters at good wages; makes hundreds of thousands of dollars in charitable donations; and pays millions in taxes every year. Yet, some are eager to shut it down. The decision about Vermont Yankee is central to our economic future and to maintaining a green energy portfolio. And it's a decision that should be left to the federal and state regulators – away from the political fray.

For the hundreds of Vermonters employed at Vermont Yankee and many more who benefit from its economic impacts; for the thousands of Vermonters whose jobs depend on our competitive electric rates; and for a stable, clean energy future, this Legislature should vote to let the Public Service Board decide the case for re-licensing.

Communications and energy factor into nearly every major decision an employer makes. In the post-recession economy, the two will be inextricably linked and for Vermont to compete globally, we must have the best of both working seamlessly together. Whether it is information technology, manufacturing, farming, education, or health care, a strong communications and energy infrastructure is critical to the Vermont economy.

Fortunately, we start this new decade from a solid foundation built through years of hard work, planning and foresight. In 2007, the Legislature joined me in setting forth a very ambitious goal: universal broadband and wireless in every part of the state this year. The e-State initiative was – and remains – one of the most forward-looking, statewide telecommunications plans in the nation. Although the recession has slowed our efforts, we have made tremendous progress.

Thanks to our head start, Vermont has been well positioned to take advantage of the opportunities provided by the American Recovery and Reinvestment Act – ARRA. While other states asked for planning funds, Vermont sought and won major federal grants for technology implementation. With nearly $70 million in ARRA funds, plus an additional $120 million in investment by Vermont utilities, we are building a high-capacity, fiber-optic backbone that enables next generation innovations to take root and grow in our state.

Part of this backbone is our Smart Grid – a breakthrough in energy conservation. The Smart Grid will help families save on electric bills by knowing the best time to use appliances. Businesses will cut costs by choosing to operate equipment when it is least expensive. And Vermonters will be prepared to take advantage of new technologies – such as electric cars – to cut emissions and clean our air.

From this high-speed backbone, we are working with telecommunications providers to build out our "middle mile" connection points into schools and libraries across the state.

The final stop for Vermont's high-speed network is in every home and workplace. This is where it gets complicated for a state that is comprised of steep rugged hills and winding dirt roads.

There are some places you can't get to from here – and, frankly, I don't want to change that.

But for families and businesses that want to get connected and are still not served by high-speed internet, I propose a "Backroads Broadband" program to spur local providers to build last mile connections. For two years, the Vermont Telecommunications Authority will delay the cost of a high-speed internet connection into the home or office. For the providers, this means a guaranteed return for a limited window and a great incentive to run the final stretch of line to every customer. This is not an ongoing program for either customers or providers – it is a use it or lose it deal that will speed us toward meeting our e-State goal of universal coverage.

For employers and employees alike, the attraction of a state wired from stem to stern is powerful. Businesses of all sizes can be connected at every hour to clients around the world. Small footprint firms can be close to our lakes and mountains without sacrificing sales. Telecommuting options multiply for everyone.

Within state government, the investments in a wired future will be pivotal in our efforts to deliver high quality services more affordably.

With each new connection, the network's potential grows for applications both public and private – helping Vermonters succeed from the office to the classroom.

The ever-growing burden of property taxes threatens the financial security of Vermonters and the potential of our employers. Getting a handle on this cost is essential to our economic future. In the last decade, total net education property taxes have nearly doubled from just over $450 million to $900 million today. And that $900 million accounts for only two-thirds of what Vermonters actually pay to support education. Almost half of income taxes, a third of sales taxes and a third of the purchase and use tax go to pay the total bill.

Containing costs is the only way to halt the climb of property tax bills and make our state affordable for families and businesses. That is why I continue to fight so hard to put the brakes on spending and to reform our broken funding system. In recent years, I called for caps on education spending, but we took only a small step in containing costs with the two-vote approach. Last year, I renewed my call to cap school spending as part of another push for comprehensive reform.

Another year has passed: ideas have been offered; groups have met; studies of studies have been studied again; but little has been done. Despite the recession and near zero inflation, school budgets are still projected to rise by two percent next year. Property taxes are slated to increase by $59 million. And for the first time since the enactment of Act 60, the statewide property tax rate will increase – by two cents – to cover ever-increasing costs, with an additional 20 cent jump over the following two years – pushing residential rates 26 percent higher than today. These facts paint a disturbing picture of a future burdened by increasing property taxes – suppressing job creation and homeownership.

Meaningful reform must address each of the three core drivers that push property taxes higher year after year. Foremost, we need to cut costs and bring spending in line with reasonable standards. We must modernize our antiquated education bureaucracy. And we must be prepared to disentangle the twisted funding system born with Act 60. We can and must change, reform and improve education funding and, indeed, education in Vermont.

Since 1997, school staffing levels have increased by 23 percent, while our student population has decreased by 11.5 percent. The number of teacher's aides has gone up 43 percent. The number of support staff has gone up 48 percent. For every four fewer students a new teacher, teacher's aide or staff person was hired. There are 11 students for every teacher – the lowest ratio in the country – and a staggering five students for every adult in our schools. With personnel costs accounting for 80 percent of total school spending, it's no wonder that our K-12 system is among the most expensive in the nation at $14,000 per student per year.

In most organizations, if your customer base is shrinking, you make adjustments to stay within budget and, at a minimum, you stop hiring. Although some will be quick to scold that "education is not a business," neither is Medicaid or public safety or environmental conservation. But in each of these areas, if we ignore the basics of prudent financial management, we imperil the services that we provide. Until labor costs in our schools are brought under control, taxpayers can expect their bills to grow every year and the onus of the property tax will continue to threaten a healthy economy.

I appreciate the difficulty of reducing personnel costs. Over the past two years, the State has taken necessary – and sometimes painful – steps to find labor savings through vacancies, retirements, and, when all else failed, layoffs. I am grateful to state employees who last week ratified, by a wide margin, a new contract that is in the public's interest. A three percent wage reduction frozen for two years is a meaningful and important contribution to the greater challenges that face Vermont.

To date, we have not seen similar agreements between teachers and school boards. In fact, teachers' salaries have continued to rise during this recession. If teachers' contracts mirrored the recent state employee contract, there would be no need to raise property tax rates in 2011.

Current staffing and compensation levels cannot be maintained as the student count continues to decline. If we simply move from our current 11 to 1 student/teacher ratio to 13 to 1, we would still have one of the lowest ratios in the country, while saving as much as $100 million. If we want to make education costs sustainable, we must return balance to classrooms.

I propose that over four years we bring our statewide student/teacher ratio to affordable levels. By leveraging the retirement bubble among teachers, we would be able to achieve significant savings through attrition alone – without any disruption in the classroom. This is not an early retirement incentive, but a mechanism to fill only one vacancy for every two retirements. Based on our experience in state government, this approach is sensible, achievable and much preferable to the alternative.

To further rein in the massive growth in labor costs, I propose requiring that new teachers' contracts establish a minimum 20 percent share for health insurance costs. State employees and many others in both the private and public sectors have accepted a 20 percent share as the standard contribution.

Our school governance structures are a vestige of the 19th century and, like our unsustainable personnel costs, must be reformed. We have 290 separate school districts – one for every 312 students – 63 different supervisory bodies and a State Board of Education. That's a total of 354 different education governing bodies for a state with only 251 towns. We spend, by some estimates, nearly triple the national average for school administration. There is no doubt that we have room to make our system of education more efficient and affordable.

A recently issued report from the Transformation Policy Commission outlined changes aimed at improving student outcomes. One recommendation – consolidating into as few as 12 education districts – highlights that a 21st century governance system can provide more than cost savings. A modern system opens the schoolhouse doors and allows students to explore new learning opportunities, in different settings, with the latest technologies.

Reforming the outdated school governance bureaucracy is long overdue. The plan put forth by legislators and my administration two days ago calls for a five percent reduction in governance spending in the next fiscal year and an additional 10 percent reduction in 2012. Streamlining services, centralizing back office functions and consolidating districts will be necessary to meet the challenge. Restraining governance spending will allow us to make investments in reforms, classroom technology and, most importantly, our students.

At the root of our education funding challenge is a system that's substantially eroding local control. Each year the connection between your school budget vote and your property tax bill becomes more and more distant. Expanded subsidies mask true costs. The budget you approve is not the budget you are billed for. And even as tax rates decrease, property tax bills increase.

This is the upside-down world spawned from Act 60. When there is confusion, there is no control. If we are not serious about reforming this system, your Town Meeting vote will become an empty action and local control will be dead. We must not allow this to happen.

At thirteen years old, our education funding regime has grown into an unmanageable maze of exemptions, deductions, prebates, rebates, cost-shifts and hidden funding sources. Overlapping rings of complexity keep all but a few experts from understanding the many moving pieces. This is not good tax policy, not good government, and, if you ask most Vermonters, not good for much of anything. It's time to pull back the curtains and let the sun shine in on how education is funded. Transparency – Who is paying? What are we paying for? What are the results? – has been a missing element of education financing since the passage of Act 60.

Something most Vermonters may be surprised to learn is that taxpayers are funding 1,000 students who don't exist. These so-called "phantom" students are a creation of our system. When a school reports its per-pupil count each year, that number can only decrease by 3.5 percent from the previous year – regardless of how steep the actual decline. For schools shrinking year after year, this policy compounds the distance between reality and what Vermonters pay for. I propose increasing the cap to ten percent this year, then gradually phasing it out over three years.

When I first went to Town Meeting, each voter knew that a vote for increased spending was a vote to increase his or her property taxes. Vermonters were generous, but careful.

As education funding evolved, income sensitivity was created as a necessary safety valve to ensure that low income people weren't forced from their homes by high property taxes. Over time – and over my objections – the program was expanded to more and more people with higher and higher incomes. What started as assistance to the less fortunate has grown into an entitlement for over two-thirds of taxpayers, some with incomes as high as $110,000.

From a school budgeting perspective, income sensitivity subsidies distort decision-making by divorcing the majority of voters from the real cost of education. Next year 70 percent of Vermonters will be shielded from the full brunt of education spending decisions. When an increasing number of voters are exempted from paying the full share, higher school budgets become easier to pass. The natural check and balance of the old-time Town Meeting is gone.

While that might seem like good politics to some, it is terrible policy. Each expansion of the subsidy pushes increased costs to a shrinking number of residents and businesses and further erodes local control. It sends spending and property tax bills ever higher – making our economy less competitive.

The push for greater expansions has also led to extreme inequities in the system. There are over 6,000 Vermonters receiving a property tax subsidy who own homes valued at $400,000 or more. Of those, there are 136 people who live in $1 million homes being subsidized.

In the education fund, income sensitivity payments are a growing, dark cloud blocking out more important priorities. This program is expected to grow by $26 million next year – a jump of 18 percent. It will be a full 11 percent of the entire education fund – bigger than the special, technical and adult education programs combined.

If left unchanged, by 2012, the program will cost $183 million – 54 percent more than just four years earlier. As the cost of income sensitivity grows, it leaves less money for important education priorities. The choice between directing education resources to our children and growing this subsidy is an easy one.

By making progressive eligibility adjustments and curbing payments on homesteads valued greater than $400,000, we can put the program on a sustainable course – preserving it for those who need it most.

I recognize that changes to the income sensitivity program will impact some taxpayers, but bringing common sense to this subsidy is an essential step to reducing the overall cost of education and providing real property tax relief for all in the years to come. In fact, if income sensitivity payments were not increased this year, there would no increase in the residential property tax rate. Our goal must be to reduce the need for exemptions over time with responsible school spending decisions and a robust tax base that allows for lower rates.

My proposals for education reform go to the heart of runaway spending and, taken together, stop the projected two cent increase, plus drop the rates by another penny. Compared against a system left unreformed, my proposal will result in $33 million in lower property taxes – a welcome break for taxpayers.

As we work to reform education financing and bring balance back to our system, we cannot lose sight of our underlying purpose: to provide high quality learning opportunities at a cost that doesn't strangle our economy, forcing our children to leave in search of jobs, taking our education investment with them.

Throughout Vermont, efforts are underway to help students who learn in different ways, at different times. We must always be on the lookout for new ways to ensure our system of education is serving the needs of today's students.

Currently, Vermont schools are prohibited by law from accessing out-of-state distance learning programs. This is a barrier to a student who is, for example, interested in learning Chinese, while earning credits toward graduation. If a school sought to provide a new Chinese program for this student, or even a group of students, they would have to hire a new teacher with the expertise – a costly step.

Allowing students to access approved distance learning programs from around the country is a simple, affordable change we can make to improve quality and increase opportunities. And it is a change that complements our efforts to wire schools and apply new technologies to the classroom.

No longer can we settle for the old paradigm that says the only way to improve education is to spend money to hire a teacher for a classroom. Instead, new thinking, creative ideas and an impulse toward change that excites, empowers and improves the education of our children must guide us in constantly reforming education in Vermont.

In all our efforts, Vermonters will judge us on the sum of our work, not the parts. They will judge us on our ability to get our economy moving again and on our ability to work together and craft a sustainable budget. If ever there were a time in our state's history for public servants to join together, and to dedicate ourselves completely to the economic strength and individual prosperity of our people, that time is now.

As a young man, 37 years ago, I took my seat in this Assembly for the first time. I listened as Governor Davis bid farewell to the office I am now so honored to hold. That morning, the departing Governor spoke of a foundation rooted in fiscal responsibility, efficient government and environmental protection. But that foundation was not an end in itself; rather it served to help Vermonters face a fundamental question he posed: "How shall we preserve the Vermont way of life?"

Like all under this Golden Dome, I've shared in the joys, sorrows, accomplishments and disappointments of daily life here and across our state. I've been a first-hand witness to, and participant in that "Vermont way of life."

I've seen it in a neighbor helping stack wood or pull a car from a deep rut in mud season. I've heard it in Town Meeting debates and deployment speeches. I've felt it on the coldest winter night and on a windy autumn day. And I've known it in the service of a firefighter, a church deacon or the anonymous volunteer just doing her part to better the community with no expectation of thanks.

The "Vermont way of life" is something not easily defined. It's rooted in a common decency and eternal hope for a better future. It's a shared love of this land and respect for one another. And I can attest that it is something worth preserving; something worth defending; something worth fighting for.

As we embark on the road ahead, let us take strength and comfort from the knowledge that others, who've come before, have succeeded in keeping for this generation the promise of Vermont. But let us be humbled in the understanding that it is our duty to keep that promise for those who follow.

God bless each of you and the great State of Vermont.

Not Seeking a Fifth Term
August 27, 2010

I WANT TO thank all of you for coming this morning.

I especially want to thank the members of my Administration for being here, as well as my staff.

Since January 1973, after I was first elected to the Vermont House, I've been making the trip over the Appalachian Gap from my home in Middlebury to serve the people in Montpelier.

I've traversed that pass at all hours, in all seasons, through rain, snow and sun. On a clear day, I can look west over the Champlain basin and east toward the Connecticut River valley, out across the breadth of this place that is like no other. And each time I reach the top, I am reminded of the sturdy shoulders of our people – as strong and as solid as the hills – and my hope for Vermont is renewed.

Through my years in public service, I have had the great opportunity to share with my fellow Vermonters their proud achievements and the joys of daily life in Vermont: the opening of a new business in St. Johnsbury, pancakes with little leaguers in Starksboro, celebrating our traditions with farmers and sugar-makers at Dairy Days and the Maple Festival, waving the green flag at Thunder Road, and helping to welcome home a local hero, Captain Richard Phillips.

The rewards of this job are many, like joining hands in service to help improve the lives of our friends and neighbors: delivering meals to homebound seniors in Orange County, celebrating National Night Out in South Burlington, marching to Prevent Child Abuse in Montpelier, splitting wood to heat needy homes in Springfield, or helping to load nearly 70 18-wheelers with donated goods bound for the Gulf Coast in the aftermath of Hurricane Katrina.

And it's an honor to be with Vermonters during their times of trial and hardship: touring the devastations from floods, storms and fires, meeting with employees after a plant closure, or holding the hand of a Gold Star Mother or Wife.

These occasions have given me the opportunity to speak with Vermonters, to hear their fears and troubles, their hopes and ideas. I've brought them back with me to Montpelier – where government has responded.

We've charted a course for our state that will bring good job opportunities, more affordable homes, safer communities and clean air and water.

I've made health care reform a priority – reaching across party lines to get the job done – because it continues to be a burden on the pocketbooks of hard-working Vermonters. We implemented the Blueprint for Health to help people lead healthier lives and reduce health care costs. Because of our first-of-its-kind Global Commitment waiver, we are a leader in forward-thinking, innovative health system reform. And Catamount Health is bringing health care within reach of more Vermonters. As Chairman of the National Governors Association I'm taking our successes to Washington to demonstrate how real reform can be achieved.

I've pushed to make higher education more affordable – through Promise Scholarships and the Next Generation Initiative – so young people can go to school here, lead the next wave of innovation in our state and create new economic opportunities.

A steady and reliable infrastructure is essential if we are going to compete in a changing economy. The e-State initiative will ensure that all Vermonters have access to broadband and cell service. And our efforts to increase and target investments in our roads, rails, bridges and culverts have been critical.

The actions we've taken to prevent and treat drug abuse; combat sexual violence; and support law enforcement, fire fighters, first responders and other public safety professionals, are making our communities safer.

I am proud to carry on Vermont's long-held commitment to our environment. We've taken bold steps to clean up Lake Champlain and other impaired waterways. We've fought to keep our air clean, even if it meant fighting Washington and the automobile industry on emissions standards. We were a leader in the Regional Greenhouse Gas Initiative, because passing along a healthy environment to the next generation requires reaching outside our borders and working with our neighbors in the region and, indeed, around the world.

And I've fought to hold the line on taxes and spending, so that we can sustain the necessary functions of government for future generations and encourage new economic opportunities. Fiscal responsibility is at the core of the Vermont ethic – as we face budget challenges resulting from the global recession, Vermonters deserve to see their money spent wisely and their government managed efficiently.

There is no doubt that over the past seven years we have accomplished much. We've seen this state through some tough times in our nation's history – and I will continue to work day and night so that we emerge stronger than before. I am so proud of what we have accomplished. And yet there will always be more to do.

The work of democracy is an abiding, beautiful struggle – just as it should be. This land, our freedom, our liberty was not easily won and so it is worth the sacrifice we must give to maintain it. It rightly demands our hard work, perpetual motion, and an endless flow of human energy and high ideals – the very lifeblood of the Vermont soul. All across our state – from armories to local food pantries, from town halls to under this golden dome – Vermonters give deeply and selflessly, each singular act of service renewing the promise of Vermont.

It has been the great privilege of my life to serve the people of this state that I love so well. I have been profoundly humbled by their faith and support in me.

But as any farmer knows, after many years – working sun up to sun down, seven days a week – there comes a time to turn over the reins to fresh arms. For me, that time is approaching. After 36 years as a public servant, 28 of those years in statewide office, with what will be eight years as Governor – and through 15 statewide elections – I will have held center stage long enough for any leader. I will not seek another term as Governor of Vermont.

My service to this state will not end with the governorship. Whether I'm in the corner office or my home office, I will always strive to do what I can to make better this great state.

But I am also ready to write a new chapter in my life. When I first took my seat as the Representative from Middlebury in 1973, I was a young man right out of college. With some very good fortune, I met and married Dorothy, soon we were raising two extraordinary boys, and now one of my sons has a son of his own – our first grandchild: Timothy James Douglas. A new generation has a way of putting things into perspective.

I know there will be some speculation as to what is next, so I want to lay a few questions to rest immediately. I am not running for President. Dorothy has a divorce lawyer on speed dial if I ever utter that crazy idea.

I'm not running for the US Senate, the US House or any other statewide office in 2010. However, for the next 16 months, I am running state government.

Those who presume there will be an absentee landlord in the corner office will be mistaken. I will focus as intensely as I always do on the needs of Vermonters. And I will continue to fight everyday to put this state on firm footing. Now is not the time to rest on our laurels.

I will continue the good work that my Administration has done to advance an Agenda of Affordability – an agenda centered on growing good-paying jobs while protecting our cherished natural resources.

This is a historic time for our state. Vermont has been hit hard by the global recession. Businesses, families and even state government have felt the impact of a shrinking economy.

That is why we must act responsibly to rein in state spending to ensure that Vermonters can continue to fund the programs and services we are all so proud to support – especially those for the frail and neediest. In order to do that, we must build and pass budgets that are sustainable for the long term.

I will continue to fight for working Vermonters and small business owners who struggle to make ends meet by resisting efforts to raise taxes to grow government and increase spending.

As I always have – but now let there be no doubt – I will fight to do what is best for Vermont and devote my full energy to guiding this great state toward a more prosperous future.

At another hour, in another place, there will be plenty of time for remembrances and time to look back. Now it is time to look ahead to the next legislative session and budget cycle, because, as I've said before, the choices we make today as our state struggles under the weight of this recession will have a lasting and real impact on how quickly we recover.

There will also be a time and a place for the long list of thank yous, but for today, there are just a few. My thanks to Dorothy for her love, devotion, and unconditional support over the years.

I want to thank my Administration for your dedication to serving the public and for making government more responsive.

I want to thank Lieutenant Governor Dubie for his friendship, support and leadership.

And to the people of Vermont, thank you for your continued confidence. I especially want to thank of you have who have offered ideas, concerns, frustrations and encouragement to me in my travels over the years. You have given state government a truly people-driven direction and focus. Thank you for the tremendous privilege of allowing me to serve.

And with that, I'd like to ask my team to "get back to work!" We've got a lot to do.